AI for Smart Students

A Practical Guide to AI Tools in Education, Health, Innovation & More

By

Anvesh Raju Nallamekala

AI for Smart Students
of
Anvesh Raju Nallamekala

ISBN (Paperback): 978-81-987719-5-7

Ph:
E-mail: ianvesharajus@gmail.com

1st Edition: Sep 2025

Published By: Kasturi Vijayam

Print On Demand

Ph:0091-9515054998
Email: Kasturivijayam@gmail.com
Book Available
@
Amazon, flipkart

About the Author

Anvesh Raju Nallamekala is a passionate B. Tech student at Andhra Loyola Institute of Engineering and Technology (ALIET) with a deep curiosity for Artificial Intelligence and its impact on the future. His journey with AI started during his academic projects, where he experimented with simple tools before moving on to advanced platforms and real-world applications. Along the way, he discovered how AI can transform education, boost career opportunities, and support personal growth — not just for tech experts, but for every student.

Motivated by this vision, Anvesh wrote *AI for Smart Students* to simplify AI concepts and make them accessible to beginners. Through practical examples, case studies, and hands-on exercises, he shows how AI can be used in academics, innovation, health, and career-building. He believes technology should empower learners instead of overwhelming them, and his mission is to inspire young engineers to explore AI with creativity and confidence. Looking ahead, Anvesh aspires to contribute to India's growing AI innovation ecosystem while encouraging students everywhere to use technology as a tool for learning, problem-solving, and building the future.

Table of Contents

Part 1: Introduction to AI

Build Foundational Understanding of AI — Its Evolution, Types, & Importance.

Chapter 1: What is AI?

Understanding the History, Present, and Future of Artificial Intelligence

What is Artificial Intelligence (AI)?

Artificial Intelligence (AI) is the simulation of human intelligence processes by machines, especially computer systems.

These processes include:

Learning – Acquiring data and rules for using it.

Reasoning – Applying rules to reach approximate or definite conclusions.

Self-correction – Improving over time based on data and experience.

💡 Simple Definition

AI is about making machines "think" and "act" like humans.

Era	Milestone	Description
1950s	Turing Test, "Can Machines Think?"	Alan Turing lays the foundation of AI
1956	Dartmouth Conference	Term "Artificial Intelligence" officially coined
1960s–70s	ELIZA chatbot, Shakey the robot	Early rule-based systems created
1980s	Expert Systems boom	AI used in finance, medicine, and diagnostics
1997	IBM's Deep Blue beats Garry Kasparov (Chess Champ)	First major public AI victory over human ability
2010s	Siri, Google Assistant, self-learning algorithms	Deep learning and NLP become common
2020s	ChatGPT, DALL·E, AI art, autonomous vehicles	Generative AI takes center stage

Field	Examples
Education	ChatGPT, AI tutors (Socratic, Khanmigo)
Healthcare	Cancer detection, predictive diagnostics
Transportation	Autonomous cars, traffic optimization
Entertainment	Netflix, Spotify recommendations
Communication	Real-time translation, AI voice assistants

📌 Real-Life Case Study

A college student preparing for exams uses ChatGPT to:
Summarize a full research paper
Generate quiz questions
Draft a PowerPoint presentation
Time saved: Over 4 hours.
Impact: Improved focus and deeper understanding in less time.

🖼 Visualization Suggestion

- **Screenshot:** ChatGPT summarizing a topic like "Photosynthesis"
- **Timeline graphic:** Evolution of AI from 1950s to 2020s
- **Mind Map:** Applications of AI across domains

Direction	What to Expect
General AI (AGI)	Machines that reason like humans across domains
AI + Robotics	Human-like robots in homes, industries, and space
AI in Space	Autonomous planetary rovers and decision-making AI
Personal Tutors	Custom learning experiences for every student
AI Ethics	Growing focus on safe, unbiased, and responsible AI use

💡 **Imagine a smart AI assistant that teaches you complex topics in your own voice and language style.**

🧠 Reflection & Research Exercise

1. **Think:**
   Which AI tools have you used? (e.g., ChatGPT, Google Assistant) What problems did they help you solve?
2. **Research:**
   Search "AI in education" on YouTube.
   Pick a tool and write 3 ways it could support your learning.
3. **Write:**
   Where do you see AI making a difference in your life by 2030? (Examples: career choice, health, relationships, creativity)

Flowchart: Evolution of AI (Describe or Use Canva for Visual)

[1950s - Turing Test] → [Expert Systems] → [Machine Learning] → [Deep Learning] → [Generative AI] → [AGI]

***

🎓 Why This Chapter Matters for B. Tech Students

Understanding the origins and evolution of AI gives students a solid foundation.

You'll better appreciate AI tools in your field — from electrical systems to mechanical automation.

It prepares you to innovate, not just use tools.
It helps you align your projects, internships, and research with future tech trends.

Chapter 2: Types of AI

Understanding Narrow AI, General AI, and Super AI

Introduction

Artificial Intelligence (AI) is not a single technology — it is an umbrella of ideas, systems, and methods that enable machines to mimic human behavior. However, all AI is not equal. Based on capability, AI can be classified into three categories:

1.Narrow AI (ANI – Artificial Narrow Intelligence)
2.General AI (AGI – Artificial General Intelligence)
3.Super AI (ASI – Artificial Super Intelligence)

Each type represents a different level of intelligence, capability, and potential. Understanding this classification is crucial for any student who wants to master AI and apply it meaningfully.

***

1. Narrow AI (ANI – Artificial Narrow Intelligence)

Definition:

Narrow AI refers to AI systems that are designed and trained for a specific task. These systems can perform one job or a set of related tasks — and nothing beyond that.

Examples:

→ChatGPT answering your questions.

→Google Maps showing directions.
→Spotify recommending music.
→Siri and Alexa recognizing voice commands.

Real Tools:

- Grammarly (grammar correction)
- DALL·E (text-to-image generation)
- Scite.ai (AI research paper search)

Key Features:

- Trained on specific data
- High accuracy in narrow domains
- Cannot adapt to other tasks

B. Tech Use Case

Using ChatGPT to generate project abstracts and summarize research.

***

2. General AI (AGI – Artificial General Intelligence)

Definition:
General AI is the theoretical concept of an AI that can perform any intellectual task that a human being can do. It can learn, reason, and apply knowledge across a wide range of disciplines, just like a human.

Examples:
Currently, **no true AGI** exists. AGI is still a vision — it's what you see in movies like *Iron Man* (J.A.R.V.I.S.) or *Her

What Makes AGI Different:

- Ability to understand context
- Learn continuously from various sources
- Reason and make judgments in unfamiliar situations
- Transfer knowledge between domains

Why It's Challenging:

- Requires advanced reasoning, memory, and self-awareness.
- Needs massive amounts of data and computing power.
- Still lacks ethical boundaries and social understanding.

Prediction:

Some experts believe AGI could arrive by **2040–2050.**
Others are more skeptical.

Academic Debate:

How do we ensure AGI remains safe and ethical?

***

3. Super AI (ASI – Artificial Super Intelligence)

Definition:

Super AI refers to a hypothetical future where machines surpass human intelligence in **every** aspect — from creativity and emotions to problem-solving and strategic thinking.

Popular in Science Fiction:

- Skynet from Terminator
- Ultron from Avengers

Traits of Super AI:

- Thinks faster and deeper than humans

- Understands emotional intelligence
- Makes decisions autonomously
- Could potentially outsmart its creators

Concerns and Risks:

- Could become uncontrollable if not properly aligned with human values.
- Might make decisions beyond human understanding.

Ethical Concerns:

- Who is responsible for its actions?
- Should machines have rights or consciousness?

Note for Students:

Although Super AI is not real yet, **thinking about it helps us build ethical and responsible AI systems today

***

📌 **Case Study**

Student Experience: Using Narrow AI in Daily Life.

Meet Priya, a second-year B. Tech student.

She uses:

- ChatGPT to understand coding concepts
- Grammarly to improve her lab reports
- Notion AI to plan her semester schedule

These are all examples of **Narrow AI**. Though they can't think like humans, they help her save time and reduce stress. This boosts her academic performance without replacing her own learning.

***

🖼 Screenshot/Visualization Suggestion

Design a **Comparison table** or **Canva-based infographic**:

Feature	Narrow AI	General AI	Super AI
Current Stage	Exists	Not Yet	Hypothetical
Scope	Task-specific	Multi-task	Beyond human
Intelligence Level	Below human	Equal to human	Exceeds human
Examples	ChatGPT, Alexa	(None currently)	(Sci-fi only)

***

🔮 Future Outlook

Timeframe	Expected Development
2020–2030	Smarter Narrow AI in all industries
2030–2045	Development of AGI
2045+	Possibility of Super AI

Emerging Trends:

- AI ethics research growing fast
- Human-AI collaboration in education and health
- AI regulation policies (like EU AI Act, India's Digital India AI strategy)

🧠 Reflect & Research Exercises

1. **Think:**

   Which type of AI do you use most in your daily life? How does it help you?

2. **Research:**

   Watch a YouTube video about AGI. Do you think it will be safe? Write 150 words on your opinion.

3. **Create:**

Design a simple Canva chart comparing ANI, AGI, and ASI using visuals or icons.

- **4.Group Task:**.

  In your college AI club or class, debate: "Should we be afraid of Super AI?"

***

🎓 Why This Chapter Matters for B.Tech Students

Understanding the **three levels of AI** helps B.Tech students:

- Identify what AI tools they can use now (Narrow AI)
- Prepare for future tech revolutions (AGI)
- Think ethically and responsibly about tech development

As engineers, you won't just use AI — you'll help build it. Knowing what's real and what's possible is the first step in becoming a **smart, future-ready AI student.

Chapter 3: Core Concepts of AI – ML, NLP, Computer Vision & Robotics

The Building Blocks of Modern Artificial Intelligence

Introduction

Artificial Intelligence (AI) is more than just a single technology — it is a combination of several core areas working together. In this chapter, we will explore the four essential concepts that form the foundation of AI:

1. **Machine Learning (ML)**
2. **Natural Language Processing (NLP)**
3. **Computer Vision (CV)**
4. **Robotics**

Understanding these concepts helps you not only to use AI tools but also to design intelligent systems that can learn, understand, see, and act. Each of these areas has its own real-world applications, tools, and impact across industries.

***

1. Machine Learning (ML)

Definition:
Machine Learning is a branch of AI where machines are trained to learn patterns from data and make decisions without being explicitly programmed.

Types of ML:

- **Supervised Learning:**
  Trained using labeled data (e.g., spam detection).
- **Unsupervised Learning:**
  Finds patterns in unlabeled data (e.g., customer segmentation).
- **Reinforcement Learning:**
  Learns by trial and error (e.g., self-driving cars).

Popular Tools & Platforms:

- Scikit-learn
- TensorFlow
- Google Teachable Machine
- Weka
- Google Colab

Real-Life Examples:

- Netflix recommending movies.
- Email spam filters.
- Predicting student dropouts using attendance and grades.

Mini Project Idea for Students:

Use Google Teachable Machine to create a hand gesture recognition model using a webcam.

***

2. Natural Language Processing (NLP)

Definition:

NLP allows machines to understand, interpret, and generate human language.

Applications in Daily Life:

- Chatbots (e.g., ChatGPT, Google Assistant)
- Translation tools (e.g., Google Translate)
- Sentiment analysis (e.g., Twitter mood tracking)

Core Concepts:

- **Tokenization:** Breaking text into words or sentences.
- **Stemming & Lemmatization:** Reducing words to their base form.
- **Named Entity Recognition (NER):** Finding names, places, organizations.
- **Text Generation:** Creating new content using models like GPT.

Student Use Case:

Using ChatGPT to generate summaries or convert long answers into short notes.

Try This Tool:

Experiment with Hugging Face's online models (e.g., sentiment analysis or text summarization).

***

3. Computer Vision (CV)

Definition:

Computer Vision is the ability of AI systems to interpret and understand visual information from the world, such as images and videos.

Common Applications:

- Face recognition (e.g., Face ID)
- Object detection (e.g., self-driving cars)
- Medical image analysis (e.g., tumor detection)

Student Projects:

- Build a number plate detector using OpenCV.
- Use Google Teachable Machine to detect facial expressions.

Popular Tools:

- OpenCV
- PyTorch with CV models
- Google Vision AI

Ethical Question
What if facial recognition misidentifies someone? How can bias be reduced?

***

4. Robotics

Definition:

Robotics combines mechanical engineering, electronics, and AI to build machines that can perform tasks physically in the real world.

AI in Robotics:

- AI helps robots learn how to adapt to new environments.
- Examples: Autonomous delivery robots, drone navigation, robotic arms in factories.

Student Use Cases:

- Line-following robots using Arduino + ML logic.
- Gesture-controlled bots using Computer Vision.

Suggested Platforms:

- Arduino + ML
- Raspberry Pi + Python AI models
- MIT App Inventor for robot control

Interesting Fact:

AI-powered robots are now used in elderly care homes in Japan to assist with physical and emotional support.

***

📌 Case Study

Real Life: AI in Agriculture Using All 4 Concepts

A group of engineering students built a smart crop monitoring system:

- **ML** predicted crop diseases from data.
- **NLP** interpreted farmers' voice commands.
- **CV** analyzed leaf images.
- **Robotics** automated pesticide spraying.

They used Raspberry Pi, a webcam, and open-source AI libraries. The project won a national innovation award and was implemented in a rural pilot farm.

***

🖼 Screenshot / Visualization Suggestion

Create a **4-quadrant Canva infographic**:

- Top-left: ML (chart of predicted vs. actual data)
- Top-right: NLP (ChatGPT screenshot summarizing a paragraph)
- Bottom-left: CV (image with boxes around detected objects)
- Bottom-right: Robotics (photo of a robot using sensors)

🔮 Future Outlook

Concept	Future Trends
ML	Automated machine learning (AutoML)
NLP	Voice-first apps and multilingual AI
CV	AI vision in AR/VR and drone navigation
Robotics	Humanoid robots, AI-assisted surgeries

🧠 Reflect & Research Exercises

1. **Think:** Which of the 4 core AI areas interests you most and why?
2. **Research:** Search for a startup in India using Computer Vision or NLP. Write a 200-word summary.
3. **Try This:** Use Google Teachable Machine to create a basic model and test it.
4. **Group Activity:** In teams, choose one domain (ML, NLP, CV, or Robotics) and present its role in solving a real-world problem.

***

🎓 Why This Chapter Matters for B.Tech Students

As future engineers, understanding the **core pillars of AI** is like learning the grammar of a new language. These concepts:

- Help you choose your AI specialization
- Form the base of most AI-related careers
- Enable you to contribute to real-world projects
- Allow you to understand the functioning of AI tools, not just use them

With this knowledge, you're not just a user of AI — you become a creator, innovator, and responsible tech builder.

Chapter 4: How AI is Changing the World

Real-World Impact of Artificial Intelligence in Everyday Life

Introduction

Artificial Intelligence is no longer a futuristic concept; it is transforming how we learn, work, communicate, travel, heal, and even entertain ourselves. From helping doctors detect diseases faster to enabling students to learn smarter, AI is embedded into our daily experiences — often without us realizing it.

This chapter explores how AI is reshaping industries and everyday life, and why understanding this transformation is critical for students and future professionals.

AI Across Major Sectors

1. **Education**

   AI Tutors: Personalized learning with tools like Khanmigo & Socratic.

   Grading Automation: AI can evaluate quizzes, track student progress.

   Language Learning: Duolingo's AI adapts to each learner's pace.

2. **Healthcare**

   Diagnostics: AI tools like IBM Watson assist in early disease detection.

   Robotic Surgery: Systems like Da Vinci provide high precision.

Predictive Analytics: AI predicts outbreaks, monitors patient data.

3. **Transportation**

   Self-driving Cars: Tesla, Waymo, and others use AI to interpret traffic and make driving decisions.

   Logistics: AI optimizes delivery routes for companies like Amazon.

   Smart Traffic Control: AI sensors reduce traffic congestion.

4. **Finance**

   Fraud Detection: AI spots suspicious transactions instantly.

   Credit Scoring: Loan risk analysis using AI-based predictions.

   Trading Bots: Algorithms perform high-speed stock trades.

5. **Agriculture**

   Crop Monitoring: Drones with AI analyze crop health.

   Soil Analysis: AI checks soil data to suggest fertilizers.

   Pest Detection: CV systems identify crop diseases early.

6. **Entertainment & Media**

   Recommendation Engines: Netflix, YouTube, and Spotify use AI to suggest content.

   AI Music/Video Generation: Tools like AIVA & RunwayML can compose music or edit videos.

   Game AI: Opponents in games adapt using AI logic.

***

AI in Daily Life (Student Perspective)

Task	AI Tool Example	Benefit
Study planning	Notion AI, Google Calendar	Organizes tasks and schedules
Writing assistance	ChatGPT, Grammarly	Improves grammar and clarity
Presentation design	Tome AI, Beautiful.ai	Creates slides with visual flow
Language learning	Duolingo, Elsa Speak	Offers instant feedback
Career prep	Rezi, Interview.ai	Builds resume, simulates interviews
Creativity projects	Canva, Adobe Firefly	Generates designs and ideas

📌 Case Study

AI for Social Good: Flood Prediction System in India

A team of engineers and researchers in India partnered with Google AI to build an early flood warning system using:

- **Machine Learning**for water level prediction
- **Satellite Images**analyzed by Computer Vision
- **NLP** models to translate warnings in local languages

Result: Thousands of lives were saved in Bihar and Assam through timely alerts, showing how AI can have a real-world humanitarian impact.

***

🖼 Screenshot / Visualization Idea

Create a Canva-based infographic with:

- Icons representing each industry (Education, Health, Transport, etc.)
- A map of India showing regions with AI-based solutions (e.g., flood zones, agri-tech zones)
- Side panel of daily-life AI tools students use

Future Trends: What's Next?

Area	Upcoming Innovations
AI + AR/VR	Immersive learning, virtual surgeries
AI + IoT	Smarter cities, real-time environment data
AI in Governance	Policy monitoring, legal document analysis
Emotional AI	Detecting mood via facial and voice inputs
AI for Sustainability	Energy usage optimization, pollution control

Reflect & Research Exercises

1. **Think:** Name 3 AI tools you use daily. What problem do they solve for you?
2. **Research:** Look up one AI-based startup in India and describe its mission.
3. **Imagine:** Design a poster for an AI app that helps the environment (e.g., tracks plastic use).
4. **Debate Topic:** "Will AI create more jobs than it destroys?"

Why This Chapter Matters for B.Tech Students

As future engineers, managers, or entrepreneurs, you will work in industries already undergoing massive AI-driven transformation. This chapter helps you:

- Understand sector-specific applications
- Identify career paths aligned with your interest
- Think beyond textbooks and understand real-world needs

AI is not just coding — it is solving problems. Knowing its applications gives you the edge to be a **smart, responsible innovator.

Chapter 5: Why Every Student Needs AI in Their Life

AI as a Superpower for the 21st-Century Learner

Introduction

In today's fast-paced digital world, students face more pressure than ever — tight schedules, academic competition, mental stress, and an overload of information. Thankfully, Artificial Intelligence (AI) is here not just to automate work but to **Empower Students** to learn smarter, think better, and create more.

This chapter explores why AI is essential for every student — not only those in computer science or engineering. Whether you're studying medicine, business, or arts, AI tools can save time, enhance creativity, and open doors to global opportunities.

1. Smarter Studying

AI Tools Make Learning Personalized:

- Tools like Notion AI and Socratic by Google understand what you're struggling with and guide you step-by-step.
- AI-powered flashcards (e.g., Quizlet AI) help revise smarter.
- Adaptive learning platforms adjust difficulty levels automatically.

Why It Matters:

- Saves 30–50% of your study time.
- Focuses your energy on weak areas.

Example:

A B.Tech ECE student uses Khanmigo to understand complex circuits with visual explanations instead of reading from a textbook.

***

2. Time & Task Management

AI for Productivity:

- Google Calendar AI schedules your study, rest, and activities with smart reminders.
- Motion AI re-organizes your daily tasks based on importance and time constraints.

Benefits:

- Less stress.
- Better grades with smarter planning.
- Balanced academic and personal life.

Try This Tool:

Set up a weekly plan using Notion AI with embedded reminders, to-do lists, and habit trackers.

***

3. Writing, Presenting & Submitting

Assignment Help:

- ChatGPT can help structure essays, brainstorm ideas, or explain concepts.
- Tome AI and Beautiful.ai generate professional presentations with clean visuals.

Tools That Shine:

- **Grammarly** for grammar checks.
- **Quillbot** for paraphrasing.
- **Scite.ai** for citation-backed research papers.

Example:

A 2nd-year student creates a seminar PowerPoint with Tome AI in 30 minutes — visual, engaging, and auto-formatted.

***

Career & Skill Building

AI Helps You Prepare for the Future:

- Resume builders like **Rezi** create ATS-friendly CVs.
- Interview\.ai** and **VMock** conduct mock interviews.
- Platforms like **LinkedIn Learning + AI** suggest personalized learning paths.

Freelancing with AI Skills:

- Design with Canva AI.
- Build apps with Glide.
- Offer resume writing or SEO work via Fiverr + AI tools.

Tip:
Build a mini-AI portfolio with screenshots of projects or skills. Add to your GitHub or LinkedIn.

***

5. AI as a Thinking Partner

AI Encourages Critical & Creative Thinking:

- Ask ChatGPT to simulate debates, ethical discussions, or generate innovative project ideas.
- Tools like **Elicit help design research questions or hypotheses.

Reflection Tool:

Use Notion AI Journal to record daily thoughts, challenges, and reflections.

Example Prompt:

"You are a business coach. Help me brainstorm 3 ideas for a sustainable startup."

***

📌 Case Study

AI-Powered Semester Planner: How a Student Boosted His GPA

Ravi, a 3rd-year B.Tech Mechanical student, used:

- Motion AI to schedule lectures, self-study, and gym.
- ChatGPT to explain thermodynamics questions.
- Tome AI to make stunning seminar slides.

Result: He saved 10 hours/week, reduced exam stress, and increased his GPA from 7.2 to 8.6 — proving that AI isn't just for coders.

***

🖼 Screenshot / Visualization Idea

Create a poster titled **"AI for Every Student" with:**

- Timeline of a student day (Morning → Night) + relevant AI tools used
- Icons for study, planning, writing, fitness, and creativity
- Sample screenshots from Notion, ChatGPT, Tome AI, etc.

🧠 Reflect & Research Exercises

1. **Think:** How much time do you spend on tasks that AI could simplify? Make a list.
2. **Research:** Try an AI tool (like Canva AI or Tome AI) and write a 100-word review.
3. **Discuss:** In your group, talk about how AI is helping students with mental health.

4. **Create:** Design your personal productivity board using Notion or Trello AI plugins.

***

🎓 Why This Chapter Matters for B.Tech Students

Whether you're in ECE, CSE, Civil, or any other stream — AI gives you an edge in:

- Smarter learning and faster execution
- Better presentations and submissions
- Stronger resumes and interviews
- Creative ideas and research boosts

By building AI habits now, you are preparing not just for college but for the **jobs and technologies of the future**. Don't just learn AI — let AI help you learn.

Part 2: AI in Academics

Explore how AI can boost academic performance and productivity.

Chapter 6: AI Tools for Study Planning & Time Management

Learn Smarter, Not Harder – How AI Helps You Manage Your Academic Life

Introduction

Being a student today is exciting, but it's also overwhelming. You have lectures, assignments, projects, exams, personal goals, and even hobbies — all fighting for your time. Many students struggle with staying organized, managing deadlines, or even deciding what to study next.

This is where **AI-based productivity tools** step in. From scheduling to habit tracking, AI helps you become not just a hard worker, but a **smart learner**.

1. The Power of Planning with AI

Traditional Planning vs AI-Powered Planning:

Feature	Traditional Tools (e.g., Paper Diary)	AI Tools (e.g., Motion, Notion AI)
Task Suggestion	Manual	Intelligent suggestions based on past
Reminders	Static	Adaptive notifications
Learning Insights	None	AI-generated progress charts

Why AI Makes a Difference:

Prioritizes important tasks**

- Automatically reschedules if you miss something
- Reduces decision fatigue** by suggesting what to focus on

2. Top AI Tools for Study Planning

1. **Notion AI**
   - Smart templates for semester planning
   - Generates to-do lists from your syllabus
   - Journaling and habit tracking

2. **Google Calendar with AI Extensions**
   - Smart scheduling using natural language (e.g., "Study ECE for 2 hours every Monday")
   - Syncs across devices, shares with classmates

3. **Motion AI**
   - Automatically plans your day around classes, breaks, and deadlines
   - Reorganizes your tasks based on urgency and available time

4. **Taskade AI**
   - Real-time collaboration with teammates on group projects
   - AI outlines your project timelines and roles

5. **Todoist + AI Assistant**
   - Smart daily task planner
   - Integrates with email, calendar, and reminders

3. How AI Helps Students Stay Organized

Feature	AI Benefit Example
Smart Reminders	"Revise Unit 3 – Signal Systems before lab tomorrow"
Personalized Suggestions	Suggests time slots based on your energy level & habits
Goal Tracking	Tracks long-term goals like learning Python or IoT Projects
Collaboration	Syncs group tasks and tracks progress via shared dashboards

Example:

A B.Tech student sets a study goal using Notion AI: "Complete Unit 4 of Digital Electronics by next Friday." The system breaks it down into mini-tasks and schedules them automatically.

***

📌 Case Study

Time Transformation: From Stress to Success

Shravani, a 2nd-year CSE student, struggled with time management and missed multiple assignment deadlines. After adopting Motion AI and Todoist AI,

she:

- Prioritized her academic tasks
- Balanced personal wellness (yoga, Netflix, walks)
- Completed 95% of tasks on time

Her stress levels dropped, and her semester GPA rose from 6.8 to 8.1 — just by managing her time better with AI.

***

🖼 Screenshot / Visualization Ideas

- Timeline of a student's week before and after using AI tools.
- A Notion dashboard with subjects, progress bars, and reminders.
- Motion AI day planner auto-filling empty time slots.

🔮 Future Outlook

Trend	What to Expect
AI + Wearables	Suggest study breaks based on fatigue via smartwatch data
Predictive Study Assistants	Tools that tell you what topic you'll likely struggle with
Voice-Based Scheduling	Plan your day just by talking to your phone
AI for Personalized Exams	Mock tests generated based on your weak areas

🧠 Reflect & Research Exercises

1. **Think:** What are your biggest distractions or time-wasters?
2. **Try:** Use Notion AI or Motion AI for 3 days. Record what changed.
3. **Create:** Design a sample week plan using Canva or Google Calendar.
4. **Discuss:** Share your AI-powered schedule with a classmate. What's different?

🎓 Why This Chapter Matters for B.Tech Students

Time is the one resource you can't get back. By mastering AI-based planning:

- You perform better in exams without late-night stress
- You balance college life, projects, clubs, and personal wellness
- You build habits that make you efficient professionals in any field

Whether you're aiming for top marks, internships, or side hustles — planning with AI is your secret weapon.

Chapter 7: AI Writing & Research Assistants

Your Personal Co-Author & Research Partner

Introduction

Whether it's a project report, term paper, or resume, writing is a huge part of every student's academic journey. But writing well takes time — and so does researching properly. Fortunately, Artificial Intelligence now offers powerful tools that serve as **co-authors, editors, and research guides**.

This chapter introduces the most useful AI tools that can make writing and researching faster, more accurate, and stress-free.

1. How AI Enhances the Writing Process

Stage	Without AI	With AI Tools
Brainstorming	Blank page syndrome	AI suggests titles, outlines, content ideas
Drafting	Time-consuming manual writing	AI generates structured content
Editing	Manual grammar and structure checks	Tools like Grammarly fix issues instantly
Referencing	Hard to find citations	Tools like Scite.ai suggest real citations

Why It Matters:

* Boosts confidence and reduces writer's block
* Saves hours on grammar, structure, and formatting

2. Best AI Tools for Writing Assistance

1. ChatGPT

* Idea generation, explanation, essay assistance
* Custom prompts for academic tone, storytelling, technical writing

2. Grammarly

* Spelling, grammar, clarity, and tone corrections
* Works across platforms (email, documents, web)

3. Quillbot

* Paraphrasing and summarizing large texts
* Ideal for avoiding plagiarism and rewording complex sections

4. Writesonic & Jasper

* AI blog/article creation
* Used for creative writing, long essays, and social media content

5. Tome AI

* Turns content into visual presentations
* Great for quick academic or project slide design

3. AI Tools for Academic Research

1.Scite.ai

* Shows papers with citations, context-based recommendations
* Filters studies by confidence level
*

2. Elicit.org

* AI-powered literature review assistant
* Helps identify research gaps, related papers, methodologies

3. Research Rabbit

* Visual graphs of connected papers
* Ideal for tracing the evolution of a topic

Example:

A student researching "AI in agriculture" uses **Elicit** to find the most cited 2023 papers, then uses **Scite.ai** to locate their real-world applications.

📌 Case Study

Writing a Paper in 3 Hours Instead of 3 Days
Lakshmi, a 3rd-year ECE student, used:

* **ChatGPT** to draft an outline for a seminar paper on "AI in Edge Devices"
* **Quillbot** to polish her language
* **Scite.ai** for citations
* **Tome AI** to present her work visually

Result: A well-organized, submission-ready document in a fraction of the time — with less stress and better clarity.

🖼 Screenshot / Visualization Ideas

* Split screen showing AI tool suggestions vs manual notes
* Citation graph generated by Research Rabbit
* Example AI-generated slide deck from Tome AI

🔮 Future Trends in AI Writing & Research

Trend	What It Means for Students
Real-time Co-writing AI	AI that writes *with* you as you type
Multilingual Academic Writing	AI helps translate papers into global languages
Ethical AI Citation Tools	Highlights biased, outdated, or controversial papers
Semantic Search Engines	Understands your *intent* and not just keywords

🧠 Reflect & Research Exercises

1. **Try:** Use Quillbot to paraphrase a paragraph from your notes.
2. **Experiment:** Draft your next lab report outline with ChatGPT.
3. **Research:** Use Scite.ai to find 3 citations for a topic of your choice.
4. **Write:**Reflect on how these tools changed your writing process.

***

🎓 Why This Chapter Matters for B.Tech Students

In engineering and tech education, communicating ideas clearly is just as important as building them. These tools:

* Help structure technical reports, papers, and resumes
* Ensure grammatical accuracy and research integrity
* Make you industry-ready for documentation-heavy roles

Let AI be your writing coach, citation assistant, and creative thinking partner. The earlier you adopt these tools, the stronger your academic and professional writing becomes.

Chapter 8: AI for Coding & Debugging

Your Smart Coding Partner – How AI Makes Programming Easier and Smarter

Introduction

Coding can be fun, but also frustrating. Errors, syntax issues, long hours of debugging — every student coder has faced these challenges. But now, AI can help you not just write better code, but also **understand it, fix it, and optimize it**.

This chapter explores how AI tools assist in every step of programming — from learning to real-time debugging — making coding a smoother experience for both beginners and pros.

1. How AI is Transforming Programming

Phase	Traditional Coding	With AI Tools
Learning a Language	Reading books, online tutorials	AI chatbots explain code with examples
Writing Code	Manually writing from scratch	Code suggestions as you type
Debugging	Searching Stack Overflow	Instant error explanations and fixes
Optimization	Manual review and rewriting	AI refactors code for efficiency

2. Top AI Tools for Coding & Debugging

1. GitHub Copilot

- Developed by GitHub and OpenAI
- Autocompletes code in real time
- Supports multiple languages (Python, Java, C++, etc.)

2.Replit Ghostwriter

- Online code editor + AI assistant
- Real-time code explanation, fixes, and refactoring

3.Tabnine

- Code completion tool trained on open-source codebases
- Learns your personal coding style

4. CodeWhisperer (Amazon)

- Integrated with AWS services
- Ideal for cloud-based coding and deployment

5. Kite (now acquired but still influential)

- Faster code suggestions for Python
- Especially useful for beginners

How Students Use These Tools

Task	AI Tool Example	Benefit
Writing functions	GitHub Copilot	Completes loops, functions automatically
Understanding code	Replit Ghostwriter	Explains each line and logic
Debugging errors	Tabnine + ChatGPT	Suggests bug fixes and better practices
Preparing for interviews	CodeWhisperer	Simulates real-time coding questions
Building mini projects	Replit + ChatGPT	Provides frontend/backend code examples

📌 Case Study

From Code Confusion to Code Confidence

Karan, a 2nd-year CSE(AI\&ML) student, used to rely heavily on YouTube tutorials to understand DSA (Data Structures and Algorithms). After integrating GitHub Copilot and ChatGPT into his workflow, he:

* Started writing clean code with fewer errors
* Fixed bugs within minutes

* Created a personal portfolio website using Replit + AI

Result: His coding confidence grew, and he won his college-level hackathon.

🖼 Screenshot / Visualization Ideas

* VSCode with GitHub Copilot autocomplete suggestions
* Replit's AI explanation panel beside a code snippet
* Flowchart of AI-powered coding workflow (Idea → Code → Fix → Deploy)
*

🔮 Future Outlook

Trend	What It Means for You
Conversational Coding	Code using just your voice
AI-Paired Programming	AI as your real-time collaborator
Automated Testing with AI	AI writes test cases and finds edge cases
Personalized Learning Paths	AI recommends what coding concepts to learn

🧠 Reflect & Research Exercises

1. **Try:** Use Replit or GitHub Copilot for a mini project (e.g., calculator, to-do app).
2. **Fix:** Paste a buggy program into ChatGPT. Note how it explains and corrects it.
3. **Think:** How can AI help if you're stuck in an exam-like coding environment?
4. **Create:** Build a GitHub profile with at least 2 AI-assisted projects.

🎓 Why This Chapter Matters for B.Tech Students

Whether you're in CSE, IT, ECE, or even Mechanical (for simulations), coding is a core skill. Using AI in programming helps you:

* Solve problems faster and smarter
* Spend less time on debugging and more on creativity
* Prepare for coding interviews and competitions

The earlier you start working with AI coding tools, the more confident and employable you become. These tools aren't a cheat — they are your partners in innovation.

Chapter 9: AI for Notes & Summarization

Don't Just Take Notes — Let AI Organize, Summarize, and Save Your Time

Introduction

Students often struggle to keep up with lectures, note down important points, and revise in time. Manual note-making is time-consuming and inconsistent. Fortunately, AI can **listen, transcribe, organize, and summarize** content in real time — giving students back hours every week.

This chapter focuses on how AI tools can help students capture, organize, and understand information more effectively.

1. The Pain of Manual Notes

Challenge	Solution with AI Notes Tools
Incomplete lecture notes	Auto-transcription and smart highlights
Too much content to revise	AI-generated summaries of key points
Disorganized study files	AI-organized notebooks with tags & filters

2. Best AI Tools for Note-Taking & Summarizing

1. Otter.ai

* Real-time transcription of lectures
* Identifies speakers, highlights key points automatically

2. Glasp

* Highlight and summarize web articles, videos, and PDFs

* Create public study notes with community insights

3. Scribe

* Records and documents processes or tutorials automatically
* Converts them into step-by-step guides

4. Notion AI

* Summarizes large content blocks instantly
* Converts meeting/class notes into to-dos and action items

5. Tactiq AI (for Google Meet)

* Captures meeting/lecture conversations
* Generates summaries, quotes, and timestamps

How AI Summarization Helps Students

Use Case	Example Output
Lecture Notes	Otter.ai transcript + summary with key terms
Research Articles	Glasp generates bullet summaries for fast understanding
Long PDFs	Notion AI condenses 50 pages into 5 key takeaways
Lab Manual Instructions	Scribe converts step-by-step tutorials automatically

Example:

A student revises 3 entire units in 1 day using summaries from Notion AI and Glasp highlights—instead of rereading entire textbooks.

📌 Case Study

Notes That Write Themselves

Pooja, a 2nd-year Civil Engineering student, found it difficult to multitask between writing notes and listening during lectures. After using Otter.ai & Notion AI:

* She recorded lectures on Otter.ai, which auto-transcribed and highlighted important points.
* She later summarized those transcripts in Notion.

Her note quality improved, she revised faster, and she was able to share polished notes with classmates.

🖼 Screenshot / Visualization Ideas

* Side-by-side comparison: handwritten vs. Otter.ai-generated notes
* Glasp highlights and AI summary of a research paper
* Notion workspace with class notes, tags, and auto-generated summaries

🔮 Future Outlook

Trend	What It Means for You
Real-time Lecture Understanding	Summarized concepts shown while the lecture is ongoing
AI Tagging for Exams	Notes are auto-tagged by syllabus unit or topic
Visual Summarization	AI turns notes into diagrams, mind maps, or infographics
Language Translation	Instant bilingual notes for regional language learners

🧠 Reflect & Research Exercises

1. **Try:** Record a mini-lecture (e.g., from YouTube) and summarize it using Otter.ai or Notion.
2. **Organize:** Create a Notion board for a subject and populate it with AI-generated notes.

3. **Compare:** Take notes manually vs. with Glasp. Which one helped you more?
4. **Visualize:** Convert summarized notes into a Canva-based mind map or diagram.

🎓 Why This Chapter Matters for B.Tech Students

Whether you're preparing for externals, internals, or viva, having clear and concise notes is crucial. AI tools:

* Reduce manual effort in recording and organizing lecture content
* Help you revise 3x faster
* Support peer sharing and team learning

For tech-savvy students, mastering AI-powered note-making gives you a huge productivity edge — especially in a world flooded with information.

Chapter 10: AI Tools for Presentations & Assignments

From Blank Slides to Brilliant Work — How AI Supercharges Your Presentations and Submissions

Introduction

Whether it's a PowerPoint, a technical poster, or a final-year report, college life demands a lot of
presentations and assignments. Many students feel stuck staring at blank slides or struggle with design and formatting. AI can now help you **brainstorm, structure, design, and polish** your work — faster and better.

In this chapter, we'll explore tools that help create visually engaging, well-written, and professional presentations and documents using the power of AI.

1. How AI Enhances Presentation & Assignment Creation

Task	Without AI	With AI Tools
Creating content	Manual research and writing	AI drafts slide content or assignment answers
Slide design	Time-consuming formatting	Auto-generated layouts and visuals
Structuring assignments	Requires outlining and formatting	AI creates structured templates
Grammar and readability	Manual proofreading	AI corrects tone, clarity, grammar

2. Best AI Tools for Presentations & Assignments

1. Tome AI

- ✓ Instantly turns text into interactive slides
- ✓ Visual storytelling with AI-generated designs

2. Beautiful.ai

- ✓ Suggests layouts and designs based on content
- ✓ Creates professional slides with minimal effort

3.Canva AI (Magic Write & Magic Design)

- ✓ Designs posters, slides, and infographics
- ✓ Includes text generator and formatting help

4.ChatGPT + Grammarly

- ✓ Writes paragraphs, abstracts, conclusions
- ✓ Checks tone, grammar, formatting, and flow

5.SlidesAI.io

- ✓ Converts plain text into well-designed presentations
- ✓ Great for quick idea-to-slide transformations

Real-World Usage Examples

Scenario	AI Tool Used	Outcome
Final-year project presentation	Tome + Canva AI	Visual slides with interactive flow
Poster for a tech fest	Canva + Magic Design	Eye-catching, brand-matching poster
Lab report or write-up	ChatGPT + Grammarly	Clear, well-structured academic document
Weekly seminar assignment	SlidesAI + BeautifulAI	Clean slides generated in 10 minutes

Example:

A 2nd-year ECE student uses ChatGPT to generate an abstract on "5G in Rural Areas," then pastes it into Tome AI to create visually stunning slides with just a few edits.

📌 Case Study

Smart Presentation in Half the Time

Rohit, a 3rd-year CSE student, had a 10-minute seminar on "AI in Healthcare." With only one day to prepare:

- He used **ChatGPT** to create a 600-word talk
- Converted it into slides using **SlidesAI**
- Polished the design with **Beautiful.ai**

Result: His seminar was clear, visual, and appreciated by both peers and faculty. Time taken: just 2 hours.

🖼 Screenshot / Visualization Ideas

* Tome AI slide deck with AI-generated diagrams
* Comparison of traditional slides vs. Beautiful.ai slides
* Canva Magic Write example generating a project title page

🔮 Future Outlook

Innovation	What to Expect
Voice-to-Slide Tools	Speak, and AI builds slides from your narration
AI Feedback on Assignments	Tools suggest improvements based on rubrics
Interactive Presentations	Real-time quiz, polls, and chat integrated with slides
Cross-platform Collaboration	AI organizes group edits and feedback in one place

🧠 Reflect & Research Exercises

1. **Create:** Use Tome or Canva AI to create a 5-slide intro to any subject.
2. **Compare:** Draft an assignment paragraph manually, then with ChatGPT. Compare tone and clarity.
3. **Try:** Use Grammarly to revise your old lab report — what changed?

4. **Observe:** Watch a top TED Talk and try replicating the design with Beautiful.ai.

🎓 Why This Chapter Matters for B.Tech Students

Presentations and written work reflect your knowledge and communication skills. AI helps:

✓ Make your assignments clearer and better formatted
✓ Design presentations that actually *engage* your audience
✓ Save hours of research, writing, and editing time

Whether you're applying for internships or presenting your final project, these tools give you an edge in clarity, confidence, and creativity.

Part 3: AI for Projects & Innovation

Learn how to innovate and build impactful mini & major projects using AI.

Chapter 11: AI for Project Ideation & Innovation

From Problem to Prototype — Let AI Spark Your Innovation

Introduction

Every B.Tech student dreams of creating an impressive mini or major project. But the toughest part is often **coming up with a unique, practical idea**. Whether it's for an IoT system, software, automation tool, or machine learning model — AI tools can guide you from **ideation to execution**.

This chapter explores how you can use AI tools to generate project ideas, validate them, research technology stacks, and even help build your MVP (Minimum Viable Product).

1. The Role of AI in Project Ideation

Stage	AI Contribution
Brainstorming	AI suggests ideas based on trends and your interests
Problem Statement	Refines broad ideas into a clear, solvable problem
Research	Finds related papers, tools, case studies
Prototype Design	Suggests system architecture and development tools

2. Best AI Tools for Project Ideation & Planning

1. ChatGPT

- Generate project ideas across domains
- Write abstracts, system requirements, and introductions

2.FutureTools.io

- Discover trending AI tools and APIs for your project
- Weekly updates on innovative platforms

3.Ideanote

- Collect and refine ideas in a structured workspace
- Best for team collaboration in projects

4. Elicit.org + Scite.ai

- Search and summarize research papers
- Evaluate feasibility and novelty of your idea

5. Trello + Notion AI

- Plan your project timeline, goals, and task division
- Use AI for auto task updates and document generation

Example: AI in Action for a Student Project

A final-year team from ECE wants to do a project on Smart Traffic Monitoring using AI Cameras:

- ✓ Used **ChatGPT** to write project proposal and block diagram description
- ✓ Used **Elicit.org** to review similar solutions and gaps
- ✓ Planned tasks on **Trello with Notion AI integration**

Outcome: Project approved by faculty + selected for inter-college tech fest.

Case Study

Idea to Innovation: The Journey of a Smart Water System*

Neha and her teammates used AI to:

- Generate a sustainable solution using ChatGPT ("IoT + ML for water waste reduction")

- Used **Scite.ai** to support with environmental research papers
- Chose **Glide (No-Code App Builder)** for real-time water usage tracking
- Presented the prototype at a Smart India Hackathon Their idea was shortlisted for incubation.

🖼 Screenshot / Visualization Ideas

- Trello board with AI-tagged tasks for a project
- Mindmap from ChatGPT with branches like: Idea → Problem → Tools → Output
- Project comparison chart (with and without AI help)

🔮 Future Outlook

Innovation	What to Expect
AI-Generated Hardware Designs	Tools that generate circuit diagrams, PCB layouts
AI-Project Validators	Predict project feasibility and success score
AI as Team Member (Auto Agent)	Auto-assigned subtasks and progress tracking
Real-time Feedback Systems	AI alerts if you're deviating from original project goals

🧠 Reflect & Research Exercises

1. **Brainstorm:** Use ChatGPT to generate 5 project ideas for your branch.
2. **Validate:** Search Elicit.org to ensure your idea is unique.
3. **Design:** Use Notion AI to plan your project roadmap.
4. **Present:** Create a 2-minute pitch using Tome AI or Canva.

🎓 Why This Chapter Matters for B.Tech Students

Projects showcase your **problem-solving ability, creativity, and tech application skills**. Using AI for ideation and innovation:

- Helps you create more impactful and real-world solutions
- Increases your chances of hackathon wins and placements
- Builds a portfolio that impresses recruiters and faculty alike

Don't just do a project — innovate with the power of AI.

Chapter 12: No-Code App Builders with AI

Build Apps Without Coding — AI Makes It Possible

Introduction

You have a great app idea — maybe a student attendance tracker, an event scheduler, or a smart home dashboard. But you don't know how to code? No problem! With **no-code platforms powered by AI**, anyone can build full-function apps without writing complex code.
This chapter introduces you to the **AI-enhanced no-code movement**, where creativity meets accessibility. From MVPs to real deployable apps, these tools are revolutionizing how students build and innovate.

1. What Are No-Code AI Tools?

No-code platforms allow you to build applications using drag-and-drop components, natural language instructions, and simple automation — no prior coding knowledge required.

2. Top No-Code Platforms Powered by AI

1. Glide

- Build apps from Google Sheets
- Great for project dashboards, inventory, attendance systems

2.Thunkable

- Mobile app builder with real-time preview
- Ideal for Android/iOS student projects

3.Bubble

- Advanced web apps with responsive design
- Logic-based workflows and scalable backend

4. Adalo

- App builder focused on beautiful UI
- Connects with APIs and databases easily

5. Zapier + OpenAI

- Automate workflows: connect forms, emails, ChatGPT, and more
- Ideal for automation and backend support

How Students Use No-Code AI Builders

Use Case	Tool Used	Outcome
Student feedback app	Glide + Sheets	Auto-collects and visualizes data in real time
College fest registration app	Thunkable	Students register via mobile interface
AI chatbot on placement tips	Bubble + OpenAI	Chat-based career assistant for peers
Portfolio website	Adalo	Personal app with projects, resume, contact

Case Study

Building a Placement Prep App Without Coding

Pranavi, a 3rd-year ECE student, used:

- ✓ Glide to create a job tracker linked to Google Sheets
- ✓ Zapier to automate email alerts for new job postings
- ✓ OpenAI API to generate resume tips

She launched her app on her LinkedIn and received 150+ student users in her college.

🖼 Screenshot / Visualization Ideas

* Glide UI builder linked to Sheets
* Workflow chart from Zapier showing AI automation
* Bubble app interface with dynamic chatbot responses

🔮 Future Trends in No-Code AI

Innovation	What to Expect
Voice-to-App Builders	Build apps by describing them verbally
Auto-AI APIs for No-Code	Easily add AI like vision or text generation
AI-Powered Design Assistants	Instant design corrections and feedback
Multilingual App Support	Apps with auto-translation across languages

🧠 Reflect & Research Exercises

1. **Explore:** Visit Glide or Thunkable and try building a basic app.
2. **Design:** Sketch your dream app on paper — then prototype it with Adalo.
3. **Automate:** Try using Zapier to connect a form with email or ChatGPT.
4. **Pitch:** Create a 1-minute elevator pitch for a no-code app idea.

🎓 Why This Chapter Matters for B.Tech Students

In today's world, speed matters. Whether it's a hackathon or startup prototype, these tools:

- ❖ Help students bring ideas to life without waiting to master full-stack dev
- ❖ Enable tech and non-tech students to collaborate equally
- ❖ Build confidence in launching apps, testing markets, and iterating quickly

Let no-code AI platforms be your launchpad to innovation — all you need is an idea and curiosity!

Chapter 13: AI in IoT, Robotics & Automation Projects

Bridging Intelligence with Machines — AI in Smart Devices & Systems

Introduction

Imagine a system that turns on your lights when you walk in, a robot that avoids obstacles, or a machine that learns from its own data. These aren't just sci-fi ideas — they are **AI-powered IoT and robotics solutions** that students like you can build.

This chapter guides you through the practical fusion of **Artificial Intelligence + Internet of Things + Robotics + Automation**, showing how AI enhances these systems with decision-making, learning, and adaptability.

1. What is AI-Integrated IoT & Robotics?

Domain	Traditional Approach	With AI
IoT Systems	Sense → Send data	Sense → Analyze → Predict → Act
Robotics	Pre-programmed actions	Adaptive behavior based on vision/audio/input
Automation	Rule-based fixed actions	Dynamic response based on real-time learning

AI makes your project *smart*, enabling the system to adjust, learn, and even make predictions without human help.

2. Popular AI Tools & Platforms for Smart Systems

1.Arduino + Edge Impulse

Train ML models on sensor data and deploy to microcontrollers

2. Raspberry Pi + OpenCV

Build vision-based robots that detect faces, colors, or movements

3.Google Teachable Machine

Train a model using webcam/audio with drag-and-drop simplicity

4.TensorFlow Lite

Lightweight AI models for mobile and embedded devices

5. Roboflow + YOLOv8

Train and deploy custom object detection models for automation

Sample Student Project Ideas

Project Title	AI Use Case
Smart Dustbin	Detects trash and opens automatically
Fire Detection System	Camera detects smoke and sends alerts
Gesture-Controlled Robot	Learns hand signs to perform different tasks
Traffic Sign Recognition System	Recognizes signs using AI vision model
Smart Farming Monitoring System	Predicts soil moisture and automates irrigation

📌 Case Study

Building a Smart Surveillance Bot

A team of 2nd-year students combined:

- ✓ Raspberry Pi + OpenCV for real-time video streaming
- ✓ YOLOv8 for intruder detection
- ✓ Blynk IoT for smartphone control

They deployed it for hostel security monitoring, receiving real-time alerts and footage.

🖼 Screenshot / Visualization Ideas

- Flowchart of smart system: Sensors → AI → Actuators
- Object detection result on Raspberry Pi camera (YOLOv8)
- Google Teachable Machine: training gesture or sound recognition model

🔮 Future Outlook

Trend	What's Coming Next
TinyML Everywhere	AI running on small devices without internet
AI Swarms in Robotics	Multiple robots collaborating using ML
Edge AI for Instant Decisions	Devices making offline smart decisions in milliseconds
Natural Language Commands	Robots that understand spoken instructions

🧠 Reflect & Research Exercises

1. **Design:** Draw a smart automation system for your home using AI + IoT.
2. **Train:** Build a model using Teachable Machine and test it on webcam input.
3. **Try:** Connect a sensor to Arduino and visualize data with Edge Impulse.
4. **Pitch:** Write a project proposal that uses AI in a real-world automation case.

🎓 Why This Chapter Matters for B.Tech Students

AI-driven hardware systems are everywhere — from drones to smart traffic lights. Building projects in this area gives you:

- Practical hands-on experience with both software and hardware
- Skills relevant for core sectors (robotics, embedded, automation, defense)
- A stronger edge in placements, internships, and research opportunities

Blend your curiosity, coding, and circuitry — and let AI bring your machines to life.

Chapter 14: Using AI for Data Collection and Analysis in Projects

Turning Data into Decisions — How AI Supercharges Your Project Outcomes

Introduction

Whether you're building an engineering project, writing a research paper, or solving a real-world problem — **data is key**. But collecting, cleaning, and analyzing it manually takes time. That's where AI becomes your smart lab partner.

In this chapter, you'll learn how to use AI tools to gather meaningful data, organize it, and extract powerful insights — all while saving hours of effort.

1. Why Data Matters in Student Projects

Phase	Traditional Approach	AI-Enhanced Approach
Data Collection	Surveys, sensors, or manual input	AI collects via APIs, web scraping, smart forms
Data Cleaning	Manual formatting and filtering	AI detects outliers, fills gaps, auto-categorizes
Data Analysis	Excel or basic charts	AI creates reports, trends, visual insights
Result Interpretation	Needs statistical expertise	AI explains results in plain language

|

2. AI Tools for Data Collection & Analysis

1.ChatGPT + Code Interpreter (Advanced Data Analysis)

- Clean messy datasets
- Generate insights from CSV, Excel files
- Create charts, forecasts, and summaries

2. MonkeyLearn

- ❖ Text analysis tool (sentiment, keyword extraction)
- ❖ Great for analyzing survey responses or user feedback

3. Google Forms + AI Plugins

- ❖ Use smart forms for surveys and quizzes
- ❖ Analyze patterns using Google's AI charting tools

4.Python Libraries + AutoML (e.g., Google Vertex AI)

- ❖ Upload raw datasets and let AI build predictive models
- ❖ No need to code algorithms from scratch

5.Excel + Copilot AI

- ❖ Ask questions in plain English ("What's the trend in sales?")
- ❖ Auto-formulas and graph creation

📌 Example Use Cases for Students

Use Case	Tool Used	Outcome
Analyzing social media feedback	MonkeyLearn	Finds positive/negative mentions from comments
Predicting rainfall in region	Google AutoML + CSV dataset	AI creates time-series prediction model
Visualizing electricity usage	ChatGPT Code Interpreter	Graphs and energy-saving recommendations
Academic survey analysis	Google Forms + AI Charts	Pie charts of student preferences

📌 Case Study

From Data to Discovery: Smart Energy Project

An electrical engineering student group wanted to reduce power usage in classrooms:

- Collected weekly usage data with sensors
- Used **ChatGPT ADA** to clean and analyze the logs
- Visualized savings trends, peak hours, and recommended auto shutdown times

Their final report included AI-generated graphs and insights that led to real implementation in their campus lab.

🖼 Screenshot / Visualization Ideas

- Before/after dataset cleaned by ChatGPT ADA
- MonkeyLearn dashboard with sentiment analysis result
- AutoML chart predicting temperature vs. energy use

🔮 Future Outlook

Innovation	What to Expect
Auto Data Collection via AI	Voice, camera, and sensor-based auto inputs
No-Code Predictive Dashboards	Drag-and-drop smart graphs and forecast widgets
Natural Language Stats	"Explain this table" becomes a real AI command
Real-time Feedback Loops	AI suggests action while data is still being collected

🧠 Reflect & Research Exercises

1. **Try:** Upload a CSV to ChatGPT ADA and ask it to clean and summarize the data.
2. **Survey:** Create a Google Form and analyze responses using MonkeyLearn.
3. **Predict:** Use Google AutoML or Excel AI to create a prediction model.
4. **Visualize:** Make a Canva poster with AI-generated charts from your project data.

🎓 Why This Chapter Matters for B.Tech Students

Engineers today must deal with **real-world data**. Whether it's IoT sensor logs, survey results, or experimental readings:

- AI helps you collect and process data efficiently
- Builds your data analytics mindset (a top job skill!)
- Helps convert raw data into clear, actionable conclusions

Let AI be your analyst — and focus your energy on innovation and creativity.

Chapter 15: Real-Life Student Projects Enhanced by AI

Inspiring Innovations — Real Projects Where Students Used AI to Succeed

Introduction

AI isn't just a buzzword anymore — it's a tool that students around the world are using to build
real-world, impactful projects. From solving local community problems to winning national hackathons, AI-powered projects are setting a new benchmark.
In this chapter, we'll explore **inspiring real-life examples** of student-led projects enhanced by AI, how they were built, and what you can learn from them to create your own.

1. Showcase of Real AI-Driven Student Projects

a) Smart Waste Classifier (Mechanical + AI)

- Built by: Final-year Mech students (India)
- Tools Used: Raspberry Pi, TensorFlow Lite
- Function: Camera classifies waste into plastic, organic, and metal
- Impact: Used in college canteen to promote waste segregation

2.Personal Mental Health Assistant (CSE/IT)

- Built by: 2nd-year CSE students (USA)
- Tools Used: ChatGPT API, Twilio, Hugging Face NLP

- Function: Users chat with a bot that provides coping tips based on mood
- Impact: Used by over 300 students in pilot testing

3. AI Tutor for Rural Students (ECE + AI)

- Built by: 3rd-year students (India)
- Tools Used: Google Text-to-Speech, ChatGPT, Notion AI
- Function: Teaches math and English through voice-based chatbot
- Impact: Deployed in 5 government schools with limited teacher access

4.Crop Disease Detector (Agri-Tech)

- Built by: Agri + ECE students (Africa)
- Tools Used: Teachable Machine, MobileNet
- Function: Farmers click leaf photo; app predicts disease and solution
- Impact: Improved crop yield and early intervention

5. College Bus Tracker with AI ETA

- Built by:** 2nd-year students (India)
- Tools Used:** GPS + Google Maps + AI ETA Predictor
- Function:** Live tracking + estimated arrival time using past data
- Impact:** Used by 400+ students, improved punctuality

📌 Case Study

Smart Water Conservation System — Built by AI + IoT Enthusiasts

- **Branch:** EEE + ECE + CSE collaboration
- **Tech Used:** Edge Impulse (for learning usage patterns), Arduino, Firebase
- **Function:**Learns family water use patterns and automates valve control

- **Outcome:** Saved \~30% of household water in pilot testing; won 2nd prize at a national hackathon

Key Learnings from These Projects

Lesson	Description
Start with a Real Problem	All projects solved practical, everyday issues
Use AI as a Tool, Not Just a Buzzword	Focused on problem-solving more than tech stacking
Combine Multiple Tools	Best projects used AI + IoT + Cloud + UI
Collaborate Across Branches	Cross-disciplinary teams created smarter solutions

🖼 Screenshot / Visualization Ideas

* Mindmap: Problem → Tools → AI Role → Outcome
* Real project dashboards (e.g., tracking app UI, chatbot responses)
* Before/after implementation stats (e.g., water saved, time improved)
*

🔮 Future Outlook

Trend	What to Expect
AI + Social Impact Projects	Climate, education, farming, and health applications
AI in Smart Campus Systems	AI for attendance, waste mgmt, energy conservation
Cross-Border Collaborations	Global student teams building shared AI platforms
More No-Code + Low-Code AI	Even non-CS students building useful AI tools

🧠 Reflect & Research Exercises

1. **Analyze:** Choose a project above and explain how AI improved its result.
2. **Research:** Find 2 more real AI student projects online and describe their tools.

3. **Plan:** Sketch your own project idea using at least 2 AI tools.
4. **Pitch:** Write a short paragraph pitching your idea to a college innovation cell.

🎓 **Why This Chapter Matters for B.Tech Students**

Seeing what others have built shows that **you can do it too**. These projects:

* Prove that students with basic tools and curiosity can innovate with AI
* Show how AI can amplify the impact of even small ideas
* Inspire teamwork, creativity, and smart use of resources

Learn from real projects. Then build your own — and become the next success story.

Chapter 16: Building Mini Projects with AI — A Step-by-Step Guide

From Idea to Execution — Your First AI Mini Project Made Easy

Introduction

You don't need a big team or fancy equipment to start using AI in real projects. Many successful students began with **mini projects** — small, focused, and creative ideas that demonstrate problem-solving and innovation using AI.

This chapter walks you through the entire process of building an AI-based mini project from scratch, using free tools, real examples, and clear steps.

1. Why Mini Projects Matter

Benefit	Why It's Valuable
Easy to Start	Small scale, fewer resources needed
Skill-Focused	Sharpens practical coding, data, and tool use
Resume Boosting	Recruiters love project-based learning
Hackathon & Internship Ready	Good foundation for bigger opportunities

2. Top AI Mini Project Ideas for Students

Idea Title	AI Role Involved
Resume Analyzer	Uses NLP to score resumes against job descriptions
Fake News Detector	ML model classifies news headlines as fake/real
Student Chatbot	GPT-based chatbot answers academic queries
Personality Quiz App	AI evaluates answers to predict personality traits
Handwritten Digit Reader	Computer Vision model recognizes digits

3. Step-by-Step: Building a Mini Project

Let's build a "Fake News Detection App" — Step-by-Step

Step 1: Define the Problem

- Build a tool that can detect whether a news headline is fake or real.

Step 2: Gather Dataset

- Use Kaggle dataset: "Fake and Real News Dataset"
- Download CSV with title and label

Step 3: Choose the Tools

- Python, Pandas, scikit-learn, Streamlit (for UI)
- Use ChatGPT for code snippets and documentation

Step 4: Preprocess the Data

- Clean text (remove stop words, lowercase, punctuation)
- Split into training/testing data

Step 5: Train an AI Model

- Use Logistic Regression or Naive Bayes
- Evaluate accuracy using confusion matrix

Step 6: Build the UI

- Use Streamlit to create a simple web interface
- Text input box → result: "Fake" or "Real"

Step 7: Test & Deploy

- Use GitHub or share via Streamlit cloud
- Demo your project with screenshots or live link

📌 Case Study: Resume Analyzer by a Final-Year Student

Arjun, a 4th-year CSE student, built a tool using:

NLP (spaCy + ChatGPT) to match resume with job role description

- Streamlit UI for uploading resumes
- Score + Suggestions output to improve resume match
-

Result: Got internship interview at a top startup by showcasing this project.

🖼 Screenshot / Visualization Ideas

- UI demo of mini project (input and prediction result)
- Dataset preview and model training chart
- GitHub project page showing file structure and README

Future Outlook for Mini Projects

Trend	What to Explore
AI + Automation Projects	Combine chatbots with task automation (Zapier, APIs)
Voice-Based AI Apps	Use Whisper AI or voice assistants
TinyML on Arduino	Run ML models on microcontrollers for smart gadgets
Real-Time Data Dashboards	Streamlit dashboards for live IoT or API data

Reflect & Research Exercises

1. **Plan:** Choose one mini project and outline your approach
2. **Prototype:** Use ChatGPT to help you write the core logic or UI
3. **Test:** Ask 3 friends to try your mini project and give feedback
4. **Publish:** Upload to GitHub and write a 2-paragraph project report

Why This Chapter Matters for B.Tech Students

Mini projects make learning AI fun, practical, and confidence-boosting. They:

- Allow you to explore interests across domains (health, finance, media)
- Help you build a smart portfolio before your final year
- Train you to think like a problem solver, not just a coder

So pick your tools, choose your problem, and start building. The best way to learn AI is to **use it!**

Chapter 17: How to Use APIs from OpenAI, Google Cloud & Hugging Face

Tapping Into the Power of AI Platforms — A Beginner's Guide to Using AI APIs

Introduction

APIs are like bridges that connect your ideas to powerful AI engines. Whether you want to build a chatbot, classify images, or summarize a document, **AI APIs from OpenAI, Google Cloud, and Hugging Face** make it possible — even without deep ML knowledge.

This chapter shows you how to use these APIs with simple examples, tools, and student-friendly projects.

1. What is an API in Simple Terms?

API (Application Programming Interface) allows your app or script to talk to another software system.

Without API	With API
You need to build a model yourself	You send data to an API and get AI response back
Hard setup	Easy HTTP request (URL + key + data)
Limited functionality	Access to world-class AI models

2. Top AI APIs You Can Use

1. OpenAI (ChatGPT, DALL·E, Whisper)

- ✓ **Use Cases:** Chatbots, essay writers, code generators, summarizers

- ✓ **Example:** Endpoint:`https://api.openai.com/v1/chat/completion`
- ✓ **Tools Needed:** Python, Postman, Replit, API key

2. Google Cloud AI (Vision, NLP, Translate)

- ✓ **Use Cases:** Image label detection, speech-to-text, language translation
- ✓ **Example Endpoint:** Vision API, NLP API, TTS API
- ✓ **Tools Needed:** Google Cloud Console, Python SDK, service account key

3.Hugging Face (Transformers, Diffusers)

- ✓ **Use Cases:** Sentiment analysis, text generation, BERT models, image gen
- ✓ **Example Endpoint:**
- ✓ `https://api-inference.huggingface.co/models/{model_name} `
- ✓ **Tools Needed:** Python, Huggingface API key, requests library

***

Sample Mini Project: Build an Essay Summarizer with OpenAI API

Step-by-Step

- Sign up on [OpenAI](https://platform.openai.com/) and get your API key
- Write a Python script:

````
```python import openai
openai.api_key = 'your-api-key'
    response = openai.ChatCompletion.create(
    model="gpt-3.5-turbo",
    messages=[
    {"role": "user", "content": "Summarize this essay: <paste text here>"}
````
````

```
]
)
print(response['choices'][0]['message']['content'])
```

- Run using Replit, Colab, or local IDE

***

📌 Case Study: College News Classifier Using Hugging Face API

A student built a web app that:

- ➢ Takes a college news headline
- ➢ Sends it to Hugging Face's sentiment classifier
- ➢ Shows result as Positive, Neutral, or Negative

Tech Used: Streamlit + Hugging Face API + Python

API Endpoint Example:

```python
import requests
headers = {"Authorization": "Bearer
YOUR_TOKEN"} API_URL =
"https://api-
inference.huggingface.co/models/distilbert-base-
uncased-finetuned-sst-2-english" response =
requests.post (API_URL, headers=headers,
json={"inputs": "College reopens on Monday"})
print(response.json())
```

📊 Visualization & Screenshot Ideas

- API call flowchart (Request → Processing → Response)
- Screenshot of Postman or terminal with JSON output
- Sample chatbot UI using OpenAI

🔮 Future Outlook

Innovation	What to Expect
Voice-controlled AI Apps	Integrate Whisper or Google Speech AI
AI API Marketplaces	Plug-and-play solutions for custom tasks
Auto-ML API Builders	Generate APIs from spreadsheets or user input
Secure AI API Use in Education	Schools deploying safe AI apps via APIs

🧠 Reflect & Research Exercises

1. **Try:** Use OpenAI API to summarize one of your old essays or answers.
2. **Compare:** Try sentiment analysis with Hugging Face vs Google NLP.
3. **Build:** Make a mini chatbot using OpenAI and host on Replit.
4. **Present:** Create a short presentation explaining API use in student projects.

🎓 Why This Chapter Matters for B.Tech Students

Knowing how to use AI APIs gives you:

- Real development skills beyond theoretical AI knowledge
- Access to top-tier models without GPU or ML training
- Competitive edge in internships, innovation contests, and startups

You don't need to reinvent the wheel — **just connect to it using APIs!**

Chapter 18: Building a Personal Portfolio with AI Tools

Show What You Know — Creating a Digital Portfolio Powered by AI

Introduction

Your resume tells people *what* you've done. But your **portfolio shows *how* well you can do it.** A digital portfolio highlights your skills, projects, creativity, and growth — and with AI tools, building one is easier, faster, and smarter.
This chapter will guide you through how to use AI tools to design, organize, and publish an impressive portfolio that reflects your talent and potential.

1. Why Portfolios Matter for Students

Benefit	Description
Shows Practical Skills	Lets employers see your actual work
Builds Your Personal Brand	Sets you apart from other applicants
Helps in Freelancing	Clients trust creators with real samples
Boosts Confidence	Visual proof of what you can achieve

2. Best AI Tools to Build Portfolios

1. **Canva + Magic Design**
   - Create visually rich resumes, project cards, and infographics
   - Use AI templates for clean, professional layouts

2. Notion AI

- Maintain a public portfolio page with project documentation
- AI helps write summaries, updates, and project explanations

3.Durable AI Website Builder

- AI auto-generates a personal website from simple prompts
- Great for tech, design, writing, and consulting portfolios

4. GitHub + AI Readme Generator

- Showcase coding projects with AI-enhanced README files
- Adds clarity and professionalism to technical repos

5.Adobe Firefly / Leonardo AI

- AI-generated graphics, logos, cover designs
- Ideal for creative students or startup branding

***

3. Portfolio Building Blocks

Element	Description
Home/About Page	Who you are, interests, core skills
Projects Section	Screenshots, code links, video demos, tools used
Resume/CV Download	Include a clean, AI-designed resume PDF
Blog/Articles (Optional)	Short posts about what you learned or built
Contact & Social Links	Email, LinkedIn, GitHub, Instagram (if relevant)

📌 Case Study: Personal AI Portfolio by a B.Tech Student

Riya, an ECE student, built her portfolio using:

- Notion + Canva AI for project write-ups and posters
- Durable AI for her personal website

- GitHub for technical documentation and AI demos

She used Canva Magic Write to auto-format her skills section and ChatGPT to explain complex projects in simple terms. This portfolio helped her land a summer internship in a startup.

📷 Screenshot / Visualization Ideas

- Canva portfolio project card sample
- GitHub README with AI summary
- Notion page layout showing AI-organized content

🔮 Future Outlook

Trend	What to Expect
AI Portfolios with Live Demos	One-click launch of AI apps/projects from portfolio
Interactive Project Explanations	Chatbots that explain your projects on the site
Resume + Portfolio Integration	Dynamic portfolios updating with LinkedIn activity
AI-Personalized Portfolio Views	Visitors see content based on their interest or profile

🧠 Reflect & Research Exercises

1. **Design:** Use Canva or Durable to create a homepage for your portfolio
2. **Organize:** Choose 3 projects and write short AI-assisted descriptions
3. **Document:** Upload one project to GitHub with AI-generated README
4. **Publish:** Make a public Notion or Durable page and share it with a mentor or friend for feedback

🎓 Why This Chapter Matters for B.Tech Students

A smart portfolio can open doors — to internships, jobs, research, or freelance gigs. With AI, you can:

* Build your portfolio faster with professional quality
* Clearly present your work, even if you're not a design expert
* Show your learning journey, not just final results

Start small. Start now. Let AI help you build something that speaks louder than a resume.

Chapter 19: Competitions & Hackathons — How to Win with AI

Turn Ideas into Impact — Competing Smartly with AI in Hackathons and Challenges

Introduction

Hackathons, innovation challenges, and student competitions are powerful ways to showcase your skills, solve real problems, and even win prizes or internship offers. With the right AI tools, you don't need to be a coding genius — you just need a smart approach.
This chapter will guide you on how to **use AI to ideate, build, and pitch** your project for success in competitions.

1. Why Join Hackathons and Competitions?

Benefit	Description
Real-World Experience	Solve real-life challenges using innovation
Networking	Meet mentors, recruiters, and talented peers
Resume Booster	Adds serious value to your career portfolio
Prizes & Internships	Top teams win rewards, offers, and exposure

2. How AI Gives You an Edge in Hackathons

Phase	How AI Helps
Ideation	ChatGPT for brainstorming ideas and user problems
Research	Elicit or Scite.ai for finding academic sources
Design	Canva, Tome, Adobe Firefly for UI mockups
Development	GitHub Copilot, Replit AI for fast prototyping
Pitching	ChatGPT for scriptwriting; Tome AI for presentations

3. Step-by-Step Strategy: Winning with AI

Example: "Smart Campus" Problem Statement

Step 1: Understand the Theme

Use ChatGPT to analyze the problem and extract key points.

Step 2: Generate Ideas Quickly

Brainstorm with ChatGPT: "What AI-based solutions can improve campus life?"

Step 3: Validate the Idea

Use Elicit to find papers supporting your solution.

Step 4: Build a Prototype

* Use Streamlit or Thunkable for UI
* Use OpenAI API or Hugging Face for AI model
* Host on Replit or Firebase

Step 5: Create Visuals & Demo

* Make a quick video demo using Canva and Loom
* Prepare a slide deck with Tome AI or Beautiful.ai

Step 6: Deliver a Killer Pitch

Ask ChatGPT to write a persuasive pitch in under 1 minute. Practice with AI voice assistants.

📌 Case Study: AI-Powered Health Monitor — Hackathon Winner

- ✓ **Event:** SIH (Smart India Hackathon)
- ✓ **Team:** 4 students from ECE, CSE, and IT
- ✓ **Idea:** Wearable device + AI predicts emergency health signals
- ✓ **AI Tools Used:** Teachable Machine, Firebase, ChatGPT
- ✓ **Result:** Won ₹1 Lakh prize + featured by a local startup

🖼 Screenshot / Visualization Ideas

- Slide showing idea → tools → final product
- Sample Tome AI pitch deck
- Mockup of prototype interface built with AI help

🔮 Future Outlook

Trend	What to Expect
AI Hackathons in Colleges	More universities hosting domain-based challenges
Hybrid Teams with AI	Students + AI bots collaborating in real time
Global Online AI Competitions	Worldwide access to funded projects & prize pools
Smart Judges & Evaluations	AI-based evaluation of presentations and ideas

🧠 Reflect & Research Exercises

1. **Identify:** Search for 3 upcoming hackathons (DevPost, SIH, T-Hub, etc.)
2. **Plan:** Choose a past winning idea and brainstorm how you would improve it using AI tools
3. **Practice:** Create a mock 3-slide pitch using Tome or Canva
4. **Collaborate:** Form a small team and simulate a 24-hour mini hackathon challenge

🎓 Why This Chapter Matters for B.Tech Students

Hackathons are your chance to:

- Learn fast and build under pressure
- Use AI tools to multiply your productivity
- Meet potential employers or co-founders
- Turn ideas into real solutions that make a difference

You don't need to be perfect — just **creative, committed, and AI-smart.**

Part 4: AI as a Subject for B.Tech Students

Help students understand AI in academics — syllabus, labs, viva, and more.

Chapter 20: AI in the Curriculum — Syllabus, Labs & Careers

Learning AI the Right Way — From Classroom Syllabus to Real-World Skills

Introduction

Artificial Intelligence is now part of many B.Tech programs across India — especially in CSE, ECE, IT, and specialized branches like CSE (AI & ML). But just studying definitions is not enough. To truly benefit, students must understand how the **syllabus connects to industry tools, labs, and careers**.

This chapter gives an overview of how AI is structured in a typical B.Tech curriculum and how to make the most of it.

1. Sample AI Curriculum Structure (Based on JNTU, IIT, and AICTE Models)

Semester	Subjects Covered
3rd or 4th Sem	Intro to AI, Python for AI, Discrete Math
5th Sem	Data Structures, Machine Learning, DBMS
6th Sem	Deep Learning, Computer Vision, NLP
7th Sem	AI Projects, Mini Projects, Electives (AI Ethics, etc.)
8th Sem	Major Project + Viva, Industry Internship (optional)

Labs Typically Include:

- Python Programming for AI
- ML Algorithms (classification, regression, clustering)

- Neural Network model building
- AI Tools like Weka, Google Colab, OpenAI APIs

2. Common Topics Covered

Core Topic	Concepts Included
Machine Learning	Supervised/Unsupervised learning, Scikit-learn, sklearn
Deep Learning	Neural networks, TensorFlow, Keras, CNNs, RNNs
NLP	Text preprocessing, sentiment analysis, transformers
AI Ethics	Bias, fairness, accountability, AI in society
Computer Vision	Image processing, OpenCV, object detection
Data Analysis	NumPy, Pandas, Matplotlib

3. Industry-Relevant Lab Tools

Tool	Usage
Google Colab	Run Python + ML notebooks online
Jupyter Notebook	Interactive code + theory in one place
Weka	GUI-based tool for learning machine learning
TensorFlow	Industry-level DL models
OpenAI API	Integrate ChatGPT and DALL-E into apps
Hugging Face	Pretrained models for NLP, Vision, Speech

4. Tips to Maximize Learning in AI Subjects

- ✓ Practice coding daily** using platforms like Kaggle or Google Colab
- ✓ Join online communities** (Reddit, GitHub, Discord AI servers)
- ✓ Participate in AI labs and mini projects** every semester

- ✓ Explore internships** that align with your curriculum topics
- ✓ Attend AI webinars and conferences** (like NeurIPS, PyCon India)

5. Career Paths After Learning AI in B.Tech

Career Role	Required Skills
Machine Learning Engineer	Python, ML, statistics, APIs
Data Scientist	Python, data cleaning, visualization, ML
AI Researcher	Deep learning, math, paper writing
AI Product Developer	APIs, UI/UX, backend, rapid prototyping
Prompt Engineer	ChatGPT, LLMs, conversational design
AI in Domain Fields	AI + Healthcare, Finance, Cybersecurity, etc.

📌 Case Study: How AI Syllabus Helped a Student Win an Internship

Vikram, a 6th-semester CSE (AI\&ML) student from JNTUK, took his **AI lab seriously.**

He:

- ❖ Learned TensorFlow to build a handwritten digit recognizer
- ❖ Used Hugging Face to experiment with sentiment analysis
- ❖ Added his lab work to GitHub and LinkedIn

Result: He received an internship offer from a startup building a chatbot for retail.

🖼 Screenshot / Visualization Ideas

- Sample AI syllabus visualized in a timeline
- Google Colab notebook from a university lab
- Hugging Face model output with explanation

🧠 Reflect & Research Exercises

1. **Review:** Download your university's AI syllabus and map it to tools like ChatGPT, Colab, or Hugging Face
2. **Practice:** Try implementing any one ML model (e.g., KNN or Linear Regression) on Google Colab
3. **Explore:** Visit Huggingface.co and explore any one pre-trained NLP or vision model
4. **Connect:** Talk to seniors or professors and ask how they applied lab work in projects or internships

🎓 Why This Chapter Matters for B.Tech Students

Understanding your AI syllabus as a **launchpad, not just a list of topics** changes your entire academic approach:

* You'll be more confident in interviews
* Your projects will be more impactful
* You'll connect theory to tools that are shaping the world

Whether your branch is CSE, ECE, IT, or AIML — this chapter helps you turn curriculum into **career fuel**.

Chapter 21: Assignments + Lab Ideas for AI Students

Learn by Building — Smart Assignments and Lab Work for AI Mastery

Introduction

Theoretical knowledge of AI is just the beginning. True mastery comes through **hands-on practice**, problem-solving, and building mini systems. In this chapter, we'll explore AI assignments and lab ideas that align with your B.Tech curriculum but also reflect real-world use cases.

Whether you're in CSE, IT, or ECE, these labs and projects will sharpen your coding, critical thinking, and tool usage.

1. Why Practical AI Work Matters

Reason	Impact
Concept Reinforcement	Strengthens understanding through implementation
Skill Building	Develops coding, debugging, and model-building skills
Portfolio Boost	Adds weight to resumes and interviews
Innovation Practice	Trains you to solve real problems with creative AI

2. Sample Assignment Ideas by Semester

4th Semester:

* Write Python code for a **Linear Regression model** from scratch
* Build a **basic chatbot** using if-else logic and NLP libraries

5th Semester:

* Use **Scikit-learn** to implement classification (KNN, SVM)
* Analyze a dataset (e.g., student marks) using **Pandas and Matplotlib**

6th Semester:

* Train a CNN to detect hand-written digits (MNIST dataset)
* Use OpenCV to build a basic face detection app

7th Semester:

* Create a project using **Hugging Face Transformers** (text summarization or translation)
* Build a mini **recommendation system** (movies, products, etc.)

3. Lab Experiment Ideas

Lab Title	Outcome & Learning
ML Model Comparison Lab	Compare accuracy of SVM vs. Decision Trees
NLP Sentiment Analysis	Use BERT or LSTM on a movie review dataset
Image Classifier Lab	Train CNN on CIFAR-10 or Fashion-MNIST
Object Detection with YOLO	Real-time object tracking using pre-trained YOLO
ChatGPT Integration Lab	Build a simple interface that calls OpenAI API
Time Series Forecasting	Predict stock or weather trends using LSTM

4. Tools to Use in Labs

1. **Google Colab** – Cloud-based Python coding
2. **Hugging Face Hub** – Access pre-trained models for free
3. **OpenAI API** – Integrate LLMs like ChatGPT or Whisper
4. **Scikit-learn** – Classic ML algorithms
5. **Keras/TensorFlow –** Neural networks and deep learning
6. **Pandas & Matplotlib** – Data cleaning and visualization

📌 Case Study: Smart Attendance System Using AI (Final-Year Lab Project)

- Student Branch: ECE (AI & Robotics track)
- Goal: Replace biometric systems with face recognition
- Tech Used: OpenCV, Python, Google Colab
- Result: Improved accuracy and reduced time by 60% over manual entry

🖼 Screenshot / Visual Suggestions

- Table: Assignment ideas vs. AI concept they teach
- Example: Confusion matrix from an ML classification lab
- Screenshot of Google Colab running real student code

🧠 Reflect & Research Exercises

1. Choose any one assignment and submit it via GitHub or Notion
2. Collaborate with a friend to create a mini-project using two different models (e.g., SVM vs. Random Forest)
3. **Research:** Watch one lab demo video on YouTube (e.g., "AI Project Using OpenCV") and document your learnings
4. **Prepare:** Write a short reflection on what you found easy or hard in your last AI lab

🎓 Why This Chapter Matters for B.Tech Students

Assignments and lab work are **your AI playground**. Don't just aim for marks — aim for mastery:

- Turn labs into portfolio projects
- Practice AI teamwork and tool usage
- Apply what you learn to solve real problems This is where theory meets creativity.

Chapter 22: FAQs + Viva Questions for AI Subjects

Ace Your Viva — Most Asked Questions on AI Concepts, Tools, and Use Cases

Introduction

Viva voce and oral exams are part of almost every AI lab or course assessment in engineering colleges. In this chapter, you'll find a curated list of frequently asked questions (FAQs), viva questions, and smart answers across beginner to intermediate levels.

These will help you prepare confidently for semester exams, lab tests, and interviews.

1. General Viva Questions for AI Labs

Question	Sample Answer
What is Artificial Intelligence?	AI is the simulation of human intelligence by machines, especially computer systems.
Difference between AI, ML, and DL?	AI is the overall concept, ML is a subset that learns from data, and DL is ML using deep neural networks.
Define Supervised Learning.	It's a type of ML where both input data and output labels are provided for training.
What is an algorithm?	A step-by-step set of instructions for solving a problem.
What is overfitting?	When a model performs well on training data but poorly on unseen test data.

2. Technical Viva Questions by Topic

- **Machine Learning**
    * What are features and labels?
    * What's the use of the confusion matrix?

* Explain the difference between classification and regression.
* Name commonly used ML libraries in Python.
*

- **Deep Learning**

* What is a neural network?
* What is the role of activation functions?
* Name three types of neural networks.
* What is the vanishing gradient problem? NLP (Natural Language Processing)
* What is tokenization?
* How does sentiment analysis work?
* What is the difference between Bag of Words and TF-IDF? Computer Vision
* What is OpenCV?
* What is image segmentation?
* How does object detection differ from image classification?

3. Tools-Based Viva Questions

Tool/Library	Common Questions
Google Colab	Why is Colab preferred over local IDEs for AI?
Hugging Face	What are transformers? How can we fine-tune a pre-trained model?
Scikit-learn	How do you implement a decision tree or SVM using sklearn?
OpenAI API	How do you call ChatGPT from Python? What is an API key?
TensorFlow	How do you define and train a simple neural network in TensorFlow?

4. Smart Viva Tips

1. Use simple language first, then expand if asked.
2. Use real-world examples to explain tough concepts.
3. When unsure, stay calm and say what you know.
4. If you used a tool in a lab, **mention it specifically** (e.g., "We used OpenCV for face detection").

📌 Case Study: Smart Viva Performance by Final Year Student

Name: Radhika (ECE - AI Track)

Preparation Strategy:

- Created flashcards of every lab experiment
- Practiced explaining algorithms using diagrams
- Gave mock viva with classmates using tool-specific Q\&A

Outcome: Scored 19/20 in final AI viva

🖼 Screenshot / Visualization Ideas

- Table: Topic → Tool → Sample Viva Question
- Flowchart of model training process (to help in explanation)
- Image of confusion matrix used during an actual viva

🧠 Reflect & Research Exercises

1. **Prepare:** Pick 10 questions and answer them in your own words
2. **Practice:** Record yourself answering a viva question and review for clarity
3. **Group Task:** Pair with 1–2 classmates and quiz each other on AI topics
4. **Research:** List 3 AI viva questions you found online and try answering them with examples

🎓 **Why This Chapter Matters for B.Tech Students**

AI vivas and oral exams are not about remembering definitions — they test your
understanding, confidence, and clarity. If you prepare smartly:

* You'll speak like a real AI practitioner
* You'll be ready for interviews too
* You'll impress examiners by linking tools to concepts

AI is not just about coding — it's about communicating your ideas.

Chapter 23: Free Online AI Courses Every Student Should Take

Learn AI from the Best — Without Spending a Rupee

Introduction

You don't need to spend thousands to learn Artificial Intelligence. Many top universities, companies, and experts offer **completely free AI courses** — with certificates, projects, and real-world applications.
This chapter lists the most valuable and accessible **free online AI courses**, platforms, and communities that help B. Tech students stay ahead in the AI race.

1. Top Platforms Offering Free AI Courses

Platform	Highlights
Coursera	University-taught courses (Audit mode is free)
edX	MIT, Harvard, etc. — Audit for free
Udacity	Intro courses in AI, ML, DL
Google AI	Official tutorials and crash courses
YouTube	Channels like Simplilearn, freeCodeCamp, CodeBasics
NPTEL	Government-certified AI courses from IITs (via Swayam)

2. Recommended Free AI Courses for Students

- **Google's AI for Everyone**
    - **Platform:** Google AI
    - **Level:** Beginner
    - **What You'll Learn:** Basics of AI, ethics, and real-life applications
    - **Why It's Great:** Non-coding course, ideal for understanding how AI affects industries

- **AI For Everyone – Andrew Ng**
    - **Platform:** Coursera (Audit Free)
    - **Level:** Beginner
    - **What You'll Learn:** AI terminology, industry use, future of jobs
    - **Bonus:** Comes with real-world examples and subtitles

- **Machine Learning by Stanford (Andrew Ng)**
    - **Platform:** Coursera (Audit Free)
    - **Level:** Intermediate
    - **What You'll Learn:** Algorithms, linear regression, neural networks
    - **Why It's Famous:** Most recommended ML course globally

- **Intro to TensorFlow for Deep Learning**
    - **Platform:** Udacity
    - **Level:** Intermediate
    - **Focus:** Build and train neural networks using TensorFlow
    - **Project Included:** Image recognition with CNN

- **CS50's Introduction to AI with Python**
  - **Platform:** edX (Harvard)
  - **Level:** Intermediate
  - **Topics:** Search, logic, probability, machine learning
  - **Why You'll Like It:** Harvard-level AI coding experience for free

- NPTEL: AI by IIT Madras
  - **Platform:** Swayam
  - **Level:** University-aligned
  - **Bonus:** Government certificate on passing the exam
  - **Topics:** Rule-based systems, ML, robotics, ethics

3. Tools and Projects Included in These Courses

Tool/Concept	Where You Learn It
Python for AI	CS50, Google AI, NPTEL
TensorFlow	Udacity, Google AI
ChatGPT API Basics	YouTube (CodeBasics, Tech with Tim)
Scikit-learn	Coursera, NPTEL
Project-based work	Most courses have mini projects (image, text, prediction)

- **Tips for Completing Free AI Courses**
  - Make a weekly schedule (2–3 hours/week)
  - Practice hands-on in Colab or Jupyter Notebooks
  - Join course discussion forums (Reddit, Discord, Telegram)
  - Add projects to your GitHub/portfolio
  - Use Notion to organize your learning

📌 Case Study: How Free AI Courses Changed a Student's Career

- **Student:** Sneha (CSE, 2nd Year)

- **Courses Taken:** Andrew Ng's ML, Google AI Crash Course
- **Action Taken:** Documented her learnings weekly on LinkedIn, added mini projects to GitHub
- **Outcome:** Got shortlisted for a summer internship in an AI startup despite being in 2nd year

🖼 Screenshot / Visualization Ideas

* Course thumbnails/logos with ratings
* Sample certificate of completion from Coursera/Google
* Timeline of "Beginner → Intermediate → Project" roadmap

🧠 Reflect & Research Exercises

1. **Pick 1 free AI course** and enroll today. Post your progress on LinkedIn
2. **List 3 tools or libraries** you learned from any online course
3. **Watch 1 YouTube tutorial** on Hugging Face or ChatGPT API and summarize it
4. **Review:** Write 100 words on how free courses help students without coaching

🎓 Why This Chapter Matters for B.Tech Students

Not every student can afford premium courses or bootcamps. But with dedication and the right free resources:

- You can learn from the world's best professors
- Build a project portfolio that employers notice
- Stay future-ready and skill-rich in AI

AI education has no entry barrier — only curiosity is required.

Chapter 24: Project Submission Templates & Final Summary**

Submitting Like a Pro — Templates, Structure, and Final AI Takeaways

Introduction

Every AI course or lab ends with a project — but many students struggle with structuring their submissions. A well-organized project report can **make a big impression** in college evaluations, internships, and competitions.

This chapter provides sample templates, report structures, and a summary of everything you've learned so far — so you can wrap up your AI journey with confidence.

1.Standard AI Project Report Template

Section Title	Description
Title Page	Project title, team members, college name, guide name
Abstract	100–150 words on what your project is and what problem it solves
Introduction	Background, problem statement, and scope
Literature Review	Past work or papers related to your topic
Methodology	Models used, architecture, flowcharts, and tools
Implementation	Code snippets, datasets, screenshots of model training
Results & Analysis	Graphs, accuracy scores, confusion matrix, etc.
Conclusion	Summary of results, challenges faced, and future work
References	Any research papers, tools, libraries, or documentation used
Appendix (optional)	Extra code, charts, or outputs

2. GitHub + Google Colab Submission Format

Why use GitHub?

- Shows professionalism
- Makes collaboration easy
- Track changes/version control

Basic GitHub Project Structure:

```
AI-Project-Name/
├── README.md
├── notebook.ipynb (Colab file)
├── data/
│   ├── train.csv
│   └── test.csv
├── results/
│   └── accuracy_graph.png
├── requirements.txt
```

README.md Must Contain:

- Project title & objective
- Technologies used
- Instructions to run code
- Demo video/GIF link (if available)

3. Project Tips for Better Grades & Internships

- Keep your project focused: one clear problem + one solid solution
- Use diagrams to explain model flow

- ❖ Mention AI tools used (e.g., Hugging Face, OpenCV, ChatGPT)
- ❖ Show visual results (graphs, screenshots, dashboard)
- ❖ Include a short video demo hosted on YouTube or Loom

📌 Case Study: Final Year Project That Got Funded

- ✓ **Project:** AI-Powered Crop Disease Detector
- ✓ **Team:** 3 students from CSE + 1 from Agriculture
- ✓ **Submission:** Colab notebook + GitHub repo + 5-minute demo
- ✓ **Tools:** TensorFlow, OpenCV, MobileNet
- ✓ **Result:** Won ₹2.5 lakh grant from a state-level startup innovation scheme

🖼 Screenshot / Visualization Ideas

- Sample project GitHub repo (with folder structure)
- Screenshot of Colab results (graphs, prediction output)
- Slide of project flowchart from presentation deck

🧠 Reflect & Research Exercises

1. **Prepare a Project Folder** using the structure above
2. **Upload a Colab Project** and link it to a GitHub repo
3. **Create a Project Poster** using Canva to showcase your work visually
4. **Write a Reflection:** What did you enjoy or struggle with in your AI mini or major project?

🎓 **Final Summary: Becoming a Smart AI Student**

By the end of Part 4, you've learned how to:

* Use AI for your **personal growth, health, and productivity**
* Apply it in **labs, assignments, and college projects**
* Find **free learning resources** and build your AI foundation
* Present your work professionally and confidently

🔔 Remember: AI is not just about models and math. It's a tool that can shape your career, creativity, and contribution to society.

So build boldly, learn openly, and always stay curious.

Part 5: AI for Personal Growth

Explore how AI tools help in mental health, fitness, sports, and mindfulness.

Chapter 25: AI Tools for Mental Health — Your Smart Companion in Stressful Times

Healing Through Algorithms — How AI Supports Your Mental Well-Being

Introduction

Mental health is a growing concern, especially for students juggling studies, social life, career pressure, and personal struggles. While therapy and counseling are essential, not everyone has access or the courage to seek help. That's where **AI-powered mental health tools** step in.

This chapter explores how AI is being used to **support emotional well-being**, offer virtual therapy, track moods, and even prevent crises — confidentially, affordably, and 24/7.

1. Why Mental Health Matters for Students

Issue	Impact
Academic Stress	Sleeplessness, burnout, and demotivation
Social Anxiety & Isolation	Difficulty making friends, feeling left out
Fear of Failure	Overthinking, self-doubt, and low confidence
Lack of Support	Students may not have someone to share thoughts with; increased risk of disengagement

2. Popular AI Tools for Mental Health

❖ Wysa – AI Chatbot for Emotional Support

i. 24x7 AI-based conversational agent for mood tracking and CBT (Cognitive Behavioral Therapy)

ii. Helps users cope with stress, anxiety, and sadness through positive conversations

iii. Offers meditation, journal writing, breathing exercises

- **Youper – AI-Powered Therapy Assistant**
  i. Combines psychology with AI to simulate therapy sessions
  ii. Tracks emotions and mental health progress over time
  iii. Helps users identify behavioral patterns

- **Woebot – Your Friendly Mental Health Robot**
  i. Created by Stanford psychologists
  ii. Offers scientifically backed techniques through daily chats
  iii. Uses NLP to detect your mental state and offer support

- **Replika – An AI Friend to Talk To**
  i. Builds emotional connection through conversations
  ii. Used by students and young adults for companionship
  iii. Can talk about stress, life, goals, or just random things to feel better

- **MindDoc – Mood Tracker & Mental Health Journal**
  i. Records emotional ups and downs with daily check-ins
  ii. Provides insights, summaries, and mental health analytics
  iii. Can alert users if patterns of depression or anxiety increase

3. Real-Time Examples: How Students Use These Tools

✓ During exams, students use **Wysa** to manage anxiety and sleep better

✓ Someone who's homesick chats with **Replika** instead of overthinking

✓ A student preparing for interviews uses **Youper** to boost confidence

✓ Users set daily check-ins with **MindDoc** to track mood and energy levels

---

📌 4. Case Study: Silent Support in Tough Times

Name: Raj (3rd Year B.Tech CSE)

Problem: Social anxiety and fear of public speaking

Tool Used: Youper + Wysa

What Helped:

- Regular conversations helped him reflect on his triggers
- Practiced CBT exercises and meditations via app
- Became more comfortable talking in team meetings

Result: Raj gave his first presentation without panic and scored well

5. Benefits of AI Tools for Mental Health

Feature	Benefit
24/7 Availability	You can access support anytime, anywhere
Confidentiality	No judgment, no fear of exposure
Non-stop Monitoring	Tracks emotional patterns daily
Cost-Effective	Many apps have free versions
Action-Oriented Support	Offers guided practices and journaling

🖼 Screenshot / Visualization Ideas

✓ Chat interface of Wysa or Woebot showing CBT in action

✓ Weekly mood tracker sample from MindDoc

✓ Timeline graphic: "Feeling Low → Chat with Bot → Meditation → Uplifted"

🔮 Future Outlook: AI as a Mental Wellness Coach

Trend	What to Expect
Emotion-Aware AI	Apps will detect tone, expression, and provide smarter responses
AI + Wearables	Smartwatches tracking heart rate + mood alerts
Group Therapy Bots	AI tools supporting peer group healing sessions
Integration with Academia	Universities recommending AI tools alongside counseling services

🧠 Reflect & Research Exercises

1. **Download one AI mental health app** and try it for 3 days. Reflect on your experience
2. **Write a journal entry** guided by an AI (e.g., Wysa or Youper)
3. **Research:** Find a YouTube video on Woebot or Replika and list 3 key features
4. **Classroom Idea:** Form small support groups and check-in weekly using AI tools

🎓 Why This Chapter Matters for B.Tech Students

College is both exciting and overwhelming. You may not always feel strong, but you don't have to face challenges alone. With AI:

- You get judgment-free emotional support
- You learn to reflect and manage emotions
- You stay mentally prepared for academics, interviews, and life

🌱 Mental health is strength — and AI helps you nurture it.

Chapter 26: AI for Physical Health & Fitness — Smart Workouts and Tracking Apps

From Lazy to Fit — How AI Helps You Stay Active and Healthy

Introduction

AI is not just for books and coding — it's also reshaping how we **work out, eat, sleep, and stay fit**. From personalized fitness coaches to diet planners and health trackers, AI tools help students stay physically healthy even during stressful academic life. This chapter focuses on the top **AI-based physical health and fitness apps**, real student use cases, and how to build better health habits using smart technology.

1. Why Students Need AI for Physical Fitness

Challenge	AI-Based Solution
Lack of time	Short AI-designed 7-minute routines
No gym access	Home workouts guided by AI videos and sensors
Poor diet habits	AI diet coaches and food recognition tools
No motivation	Gamified fitness and habit tracking apps

2. Top AI Tools for Fitness and Physical Health

1. **Freeletics AI** – Smart Personal Fitness Coach
   - Offers personalized bodyweight workouts using AI
   - Adapts to your performance and schedule
   - Needs no equipment — ideal for hostel life

2. Fitbod AI – Gym Workout Generator

- Uses machine learning to generate strength training plans
- Considers your fitness level, muscle fatigue, and goals
- Tracks progress and adjusts weekly

3. Google Fit + Health Connect AI

- Tracks daily steps, heart rate, sleep, and breathing
- Syncs with other devices for holistic wellness data
- Sends reminders to walk, move, and relax

4. Vi Trainer – AI Running Coach

- Real-time audio feedback during running or jogging
- Adjusts pacing, endurance, and breathing
- Ideal for students preparing for sports or active routines

5. MyFitnessPal + AI Features

- Tracks meals, calories, and nutrition using photo recognition
- Recommends balanced meals and water reminders
- Works with smartwatch and phone sensors

3. Real-Time Examples: Students Getting Fit with AI

- ➢ A student in 2nd year CSE uses **Freeletics** daily for 20 minutes and has improved flexibility and focus
- ➢ A hostel group set **step goals** using **Google Fit** and gamified it among friends
- ➢ Before campus placements, a final-year student followed a **Fitbod routine** to improve posture and confidence

📌 Case Study: Turning Sedentary Life Around with AI

* **Name:** Kavya (ECE, 2nd Year)
* **Problem:** Sedentary lifestyle and low energy
* **Solution Used:** Google Fit + Vi Trainer + Freeletics

Result:

- Lost 4 kg in 2 months
- Gained more daily energy and focus
- Started sleeping better and joined college dance club

🖼 Screenshot / Visualization Ideas

- Step count tracker from Google Fit
- Personalized routine screen from Fitbod or Freeletics
- Calorie recognition interface from MyFitnessPal

🔮 Future Outlook: AI and Your Body — What's Coming

Trend	Future Possibility
AI + Wearable Biosensors	Continuous glucose and stress monitoring via skin patches
AI-Powered Virtual Gyms	Real-time 3D tracking with smart mirrors and posture correction
Gamified AI Workouts	Augmented Reality fitness with leaderboards
AI + Diet Personalization	Genetic-based food suggestions using AI insights

🧠 Reflect & Research Exercises

1. **Install a fitness tracking app** and log 1 week of activity
2. **Try a 7-minute AI-guided workout** and reflect on energy levels after
3. **Use MyFitnessPal or Google Lens** to analyze your lunch and nutrition
4. **Write 5 habits** you can automate with AI health apps (e.g., water reminders, steps)

🎓 Why This Chapter Matters for B.Tech Students

Staying physically active boosts:

* Brain function and memory (good for exams!)
* Emotional well-being
* Self-confidence in social and career events

You don't need to go to a gym. With AI, your **body gets smarter** along with your brain.

Chapter 27: AI Coaches for Sports — Enhance Your Game with Smart Feedback

From Playground to Podium — How AI Makes You a Better Athlete

Introduction

Whether you play cricket, football, badminton, or just enjoy running, AI is becoming your **digital coach** — analyzing your moves, correcting your form, and helping you improve like a pro.

In this chapter, you'll explore how AI is revolutionizing **student sports, athletics, and fitness training**, even for beginners.

1. Why Use AI in Sports and Games?

Challenge	AI-Based Solution
No personal coach	AI tracks your form and gives corrections
Lack of performance data	Provides metrics: speed, accuracy, posture, endurance
No training feedback	Instant reviews via camera and sensors
Fear of judgment	Train privately and improve confidently

|

2. Top AI Sports Coaching Tools

a) HomeCourt AI** – Basketball & Fitness Coaching

- Analyzes shooting form using phone camera
- Tracks speed, release angle, and accuracy
- Used by NBA athletes and students alike

b) Jogo.ai – AI for Football Training

- Wearable sensors track ball control, dribbling, movement
- Gives real-time performance feedback
- Ideal for college teams and solo practice

c) SwingVision AI** – For Tennis and Racket Sports

- AI camera analyzes footwork, swing, serve speed
- Generates heatmaps of movement and return zones
- Supported by Apple and used by pro athletes

d) Zone7 – Injury Prevention with AI

- Uses biomechanics and activity data to predict injury risks
- Great for athletes training daily or recovering from strain

e) Move.ai – Markerless Motion Tracking

- Tracks full-body movement using video (no wearables needed)
- Gives precise posture and coordination analysis
- Used in dance, martial arts, sports fitness

3. Real-Time Examples: Students and Sports with AI

- A student captain uses **HomeCourt** to train his college basketball team
- A football player in 1st year B.Tech logs 10 drills a week with **Jogo.ai**
- A tennis enthusiast corrects their posture using **SwingVision** and improved match performance

📌 Case Study: AI-Powered Comeback

Name: Arjun (Mechanical Engineering, 4th Year)

Sport: Football winger; sidelined by injury

Tool Used: Zone7 + Move.ai

How It Helped:

- Identified risky footwork patterns
- Reduced injury recurrence
- Gained confidence to return to training safely

Result: Arjun now plays again and assists in fitness planning for juniors

🖼 Screenshot / Visualization Ideas

* Sample shot map from HomeCourt AI
* Jogo.ai dashboard showing football stats
* Move.ai analysis video clip of posture correction

🔮 Future Outlook: AI in Sports and Training

Trend	What to Expect
AI in College Teams	AI fitness programs as part of campus sports clubs
AI Referees	Smart judging in events and tournaments
Virtual Training Rooms	3D practice simulations using VR + AI
Emotion-Aware Performance AI	Track confidence and stress before games

🧠 Reflect & Research Exercises

1. **Choose one sport you enjoy**. Search for an AI coaching tool in that sport
2. **Watch 2 videos** of how athletes train using AI (YouTube/Instagram Reels)
3. **Try to record your posture** while playing/running and use Move.ai for feedback
4. **Interview a teammate/coach:** Ask how they track progress and suggest AI tools

🎓 Why This Chapter Matters for B.Tech Students

Sports boost energy, teamwork, and stress relief. With AI:

*You train smarter, not just harder
*You prevent injuries and recover faster
*You develop discipline and strategy — essential for both academics and life

🏅 Let AI make you faster, stronger, and more focused — on and off the field.

Chapter 28: Meditation & Productivity — Find Focus Through AI

Mind Over Machine — How AI Helps You Stay Calm, Focused, and Creative

Introduction

Between assignments, social media, sleepless nights, and pressure to succeed, today's students are more distracted than ever. But what if AI could guide your breathing, track your focus, and create the right environment for deep work?
This chapter introduces **AI tools that support mindfulness, meditation, and productivity** — so you can study better, feel calmer, and unlock creative energy.

1. Why Students Need Meditation + Focus Tools

Problem	AI-Based Benefit
Mental fatigue	Guided meditation and brain relaxation
Procrastination	Focus timers with productivity coaching
Screen overload	AI-driven light/music adjustments for attention
Stress before exams/interviews	Calming sounds and breathing cues

2. Top AI Tools for Meditation and Productivity

❖ **Headspace AI** – Mindfulness for Students**

- Offers meditation sessions tailored to anxiety, sleep, and focus
- Uses machine learning to recommend routines
- Short 5-minute resets during study breaks

❖ **Brain.fm** – AI Music to Focus**

- Creates AI-generated music that enhances brainwave activity
- Choose Focus, Relax, Sleep, or Creativity modes
- Scientifically tested on productivity and mental clarity

❖ **Flowtime – AI-Powered Focus Timer**

- Tracks heart rate, attention span, and productivity intervals
- Works with wearables or phone sensors
- Gives reports and suggestions to improve study habits

❖ **Aura AI – Personalized Wellness Companion**

- Offers breathing exercises, motivational stories, and emotional check-ins
- AI adapts daily to your mood and energy levels
- Great for winding down before sleep or a big day

❖ **Endel – Adaptive Soundscapes**

- Creates real-time sound environments that match your focus cycle
- Integrates with Apple Health for smart energy syncing
- Helps with both deep work and calm recovery

3. Real-Time Student Scenarios

* A 1st-year student uses **Headspace** every morning for 10 mins to feel centered
* Final-year project group uses **Brain.fm** during coding sprints for better flow
* A nervous speaker uses **Aura AI**'s calming routine before a seminar
* **Flowtime** helps students prepare better for 25-min Pomodoro study blocks

📌 Case Study: From Overwhelmed to Organized

Name: Sneha (IT, 3rd Year)

Problem: Burnout from managing classes + coding + startup

Tools Used: Flowtime + Brain.fm + Headspace

Results:

- Improved study efficiency by 40% (based on app logs)
- Felt calmer before presentations
- Reduced screen-induced headaches and sleep issues

🖼 Screenshot / Visualization Ideas

✓ Flowtime report dashboard
✓ Headspace meditation streak badge
✓ Brain.fm timer interface during study

🔮 Future Outlook: Mindfulness + AI = Mental Clarity

Innovation Area	Future Possibility
Emotion Detection	AI will detect mood via webcam or audio
Personalized Workflows	AI adjusts tasks and breaks based on stress level
Smart Campus Environments	Light, music, and temperature adapting via AI to improve focus
AI-Based Career Burnout Alerts	AI warns you when to rest based on work volume and emotion patterns

🧠 Reflect & Research Exercises

1. **Try a 3-day meditation challenge** using Headspace or Aura AI
2. **Write a journal entry** after using Brain.fm during study
3. **Research:** Look up one AI music app and compare it with YouTube Lo-Fi
4. **Challenge yourself:** Use Flowtime + Pomodoro for a full assignment cycle

🎓 Why This Chapter Matters for B.Tech Students

You don't just need tools to **think harder** — you need tools to **think better**. Meditation and productivity AI help you:

*Avoid burnout
*Stay mentally sharp
*Maximize creative and academic performance

With AI, your mind becomes your **strongest resource**.

Part 6: AI in Creative Thinking & Careers

Use AI to build a portfolio, generate ideas, freelance, and prepare for jobs.

Chapter 29: Using AI to Generate New Business or Startup Ideas

Think Big with AI — Turning Ideas into Startups

Introduction

Every big business starts with a single idea. But how do you come up with that idea? AI can now help students become **entrepreneurs** by generating startup ideas, testing business models, and analyzing trends.

In this chapter, we'll explore how to use AI to spark innovation and turn your skills into a **business opportunity**.

1. Why Use AI for Startup Ideation?

Challenge	AI-Powered Solution
Don't know where to start	ChatGPT prompts for idea brainstorming
Need help validating an idea	AI tools like ValidatorAI or BizIdeasGPT simulate market tests
Struggle with trends and demands	Trend tools like Exploding Topics, FutureTools.io highlight gaps
Building product mockups is hard	Canva AI, Uizard, or Tome AI for quick visuals

2. Top AI Tools for Business Idea Generation

a) ChatGPT – AI Brainstorming Partner

* Ask it: "Suggest 5 startup ideas in the edtech field for college students"
* It can also help define your USP, audience, pricing models

b) ValidatorAI – Idea Feasibility Tool

* Enter your idea; it tells you if it's likely to succeed or not
* Suggests improvements, features, and potential market risks

c) FutureTools.io – Discover AI Tools by Use Case

* Helps explore industry-specific tools to inspire product building
* Updates regularly with new innovations

d) Ideanote – Innovation Management Platform

* Collect feedback from peers, mentors
* AI clusters ideas into themes and predicts promising ones

e) Canva AI / Tome AI – Prototype and Present

* Instantly generate pitch decks, product mockups, and branding
* Perfect for hackathons or startup competitions

Real Student Use: From Idea to MVP

- ✓ A B.Tech student asked ChatGPT for ideas and launched a prototype for a **hostel food delivery app** using Glide (no-code tool)
- ✓ A 3rd-year student used **ValidatorAI** to test an edtech platform idea and pitched it in a national innovation event
- ✓ Final-year CSE student created a **startup pitch deck in Tome AI** and shared it with investors during a campus startup summit

📌 Case Study: AI-Powered Entrepreneurship

Name: Avani (IT, Final Year)

Startup Idea: A habit-tracking app for students using gamification

Tools Used: ChatGPT (brainstorming), Canva AI (branding), ValidatorAI (validation)

Outcome:

- App prototype selected for incubation by a local startup accelerator
- Won 2nd place in inter-college pitch competition

🖼 Screenshot / Visualization Ideas

- ❖ ChatGPT prompt and output for startup idea
- ❖ Canva AI screen of branding toolkit
- ❖ Tome AI-generated pitch deck slide

🔮 Future Outlook: AI x Startup Culture

Trend	Future Possibility
AI as a Co-founder	Business planning, competitor analysis, marketing strategies
AI-Powered Marketplaces	Tools that match problems with existing solutions
Idea-to-App in a Day	Generative UI, instant backend, and payment integration
Student-led AI Incubators	College startup cells run with help from AI project mentors

🧠 Reflect & Research Exercises

1. **Ask ChatGPT to generate 10 startup ideas** in a field you're interested in
2. **Use ValidatorAI** on one idea and note its suggestions
3. **Create a basic pitch deck** using Tome AI or Canva
4. **Interview an entrepreneur** and ask how they validate ideas (compare with AI)

🎓 Why This Chapter Matters for B.Tech Students

You don't need to wait for a job to start creating impact. With AI, you can:

* Generate ideas in minutes
* Validate them without expensive research
* Build prototypes without coding

💼 Start building the **future company** your future self would thank you for.

Chapter 30: AI for Portfolio Building — Showcasing Your Talents with AI Tools

From Hidden Skills to Highlight Reel — Building a Smart Portfolio with A

Introduction

A strong portfolio helps students stand out in a crowd of resumes. Whether you're applying for internships, jobs, or research roles, showcasing your work creatively and professionally is key.
In this chapter, you'll learn how to use AI tools to **create, design, organize, and present** your portfolio — even if you're just starting out.

1. Why Portfolios Matter for Students

Situation	How AI-Powered Portfolios Help
Applying for internships	AI-generated resumes and project galleries
Freelance gigs or side income	Build proof of work using visuals, testimonials
Personal branding	Showcase creativity, coding, design, or writing skills
Lack of design skills	Use AI to build beautiful, clean templates

2. Top AI Tools for Portfolio Creation

➢ **Canva AI – Visual Portfolios Made Easy**

* Drag-and-drop design with resume, infographic, and portfolio templates
* AI suggests layout improvements and content based on role

- **Notion + AI – Dynamic Personal Portfolio Site**

  * Embed projects, blogs, certifications, and timelines
  * Use Notion AI for content summaries, tone adjustment, and quick edits

- **Copy.ai – Portfolio Descriptions & Bios**
  * Write crisp, role-specific project descriptions
  * Generate "About Me" sections based on your tone and goal

- **Pika Labs / Runway AI – Video Portfolios**
  * Create AI-powered project walkthroughs, animations, or demos
  * Ideal for creative students, app developers, content creators

- **GitHub Copilot + Replit – Code Projects with AI Docs**
  * Use AI to build real mini-projects with documentation
  * Host your work and link it in your portfolio

Real Student Examples

- ✓ A 2nd-year ECE student used **Notion AI** to create a smart, scrollable resume page
- ✓ A final-year CS student added **Pika Labs videos** to explain their ML projects
- ✓ A creative writing student used **Copy.ai** to write project intros and get freelance gigs

📌 Case Study: Smart Portfolio, Smarter Results

Name: Ayaan (ECE, 3rd Year)

Challenge: Didn't know how to present IoT projects for campus placement

Tools Used: Canva AI, GitHub Copilot, Notion

Outcome:

- Created an interactive portfolio linked in resume
- Was shortlisted by 3 companies within 2 months

🖼 Screenshot / Visualization Ideas

- Portfolio homepage made with Notion AI
- Canva portfolio template preview
- GitHub project with AI-generated documentation

🔮 Future Outlook: AI + Portfolio = Next-Level Branding

Innovation Area	Future Possibility
AI-Analyzed Portfolios	Companies use AI to pre-screen portfolios
Auto-Updating Portfolios	AI pulls recent work from GitHub/LinkedIn automatically
Multimedia First Impressions	AI video introductions instead of cover letters
VR/AR Portfolios	Immersive demos using mixed reality and AI narration

🧠 Reflect & Research Exercises

1. **Use Canva or Notion** to create a 1-page project showcase
2. **Write a bio using Copy.ai** — tweak it to sound confident and clear
3. **Record a project walkthrough** (video or screen recording) and try editing with AI tools
4. **Ask ChatGPT:** "What projects should I include in a tech/creative portfolio?"

🎓 Why This Chapter Matters for B.Tech Students

Your portfolio speaks before you do. Whether you're a coder, designer, analyst, or creative —

* AI tools make your work look professional
* You can build fast, without hiring a designer
* It gives you confidence when applying or networking

📌 With AI, your talent becomes visible — and unforgettable.

Chapter 31: AI in Resume Writing & Job Prep — Get Noticed, Get Hired

Your First Job, Powered by AI — Smarter Applications, Stronger Confidence

Introduction

Applying for internships or your first job can feel intimidating. From writing resumes to preparing for interviews, it's easy to get overwhelmed. That's where AI steps in as your **career preparation assistant** — optimizing resumes, simulating interviews, and making you job-ready.

This chapter will show how you can use AI to **present your skills professionally, prep smarter, and boost your hiring chances.**

1. Common Struggles in Job Prep — Solved by AI

Student Challenge	AI-Powered Help
Writing strong resumes	Resume builders like Rezi, Kickresume, Teal
Nervous about interviews	Interview simulators like Interview.ai, Yoodli
Don't know what to include	ChatGPT prompts and auto-generated summaries
Weak LinkedIn profiles	AI-based profile suggestions via Resume Worded, Teal, etc.

2. Top AI Tools for Resume & Interview Prep

Kickresume – Smart Resume and Cover Letter Builder

- Templates and tone matching based on job roles
- Grammar and keyword optimization powered by AI

Rezi AI – Resume Optimizer

- Creates ATS (Applicant Tracking System) friendly resumes

- ➢ Customizes resumes for specific job descriptions

Interview\.ai / Yoodli – Practice Interviews with Feedback

- ➢ Simulate real interviews with voice/video analysis
- ➢ Get real-time tips on body language, tone, and timing

ChatGPT for Job Prep

- ➢ Generate answers to tricky questions
- ➢ Roleplay as the interviewer to practice dialogue

Teal HQ – LinkedIn and Resume Improvement

- ➢ Suggests profile upgrades
- ➢ Tracks job applications and tailors resumes automatically

Real Student Scenarios

- ✓ A B.Tech CSE student used **Rezi** to build a custom resume for a data analyst role
- ✓ A fresher in ECE practiced interviews on **Yoodli** and improved speaking confidence
- ✓ A 3rd-year student used **ChatGPT** to write bullet points for projects

📌 Case Study: AI-Driven Job Prep Success

Name: Priya (EEE, Final Year)

Goal: Placement in an MNC as a systems engineer

Tools Used: Kickresume + Interview\.ai + ChatGPT

Results:

- Got selected in 2nd round of campus interviews
- Reported higher clarity and less nervousness during interviews

🖼 Screenshot / Visualization Ideas

- Resume created using Rezi or Kickresume

* Yoodli feedback report for mock interview
* Teal HQ job tracking dashboard

🔮 Future Outlook: AI and Career Preparation

Innovation Area	Future Possibility
Voice + Emotion AI	Detect confidence and stress levels in mock interviews
Smart Resume Generators	Real-time updates for your resume based on job market data
Interview Avatars	AI avatars conduct realistic interviews with emotion detection
Job Coach Bots	Bots guide your application, follow-up, and negotiation process

🧠 Reflect & Research Exercises

- **Use Rezi or Kickresume** to build a role-specific resume
- **Try Interview\.ai or Yoodli** for a 10-min mock interview
- **Ask ChatGPT:** "Write a cover letter for a job at \[company] for a \[role]"
- **Analyze your LinkedIn profile** using Teal or Resume Worded

🎓 Why This Chapter Matters for B.Tech Students

You've done the projects. Learned the tools. Now, it's time to tell the world — professionally.

* AI makes your resume smarter
* Your interviews sharper
* Your confidence stronger

💼 Let AI help you not just get noticed — but get hired.

Chapter 32: Freelancing with AI Skills — Turning Your Knowledge into Income

Be Your Own Boss — How AI Helps You Freelance Smarter and Earn Faster

Introduction

What if your skills could start earning for you before graduation? Freelancing is a powerful way for B.Tech students to gain real-world experience, build income, and expand professional networks. And now, with AI tools, even beginners can deliver high-quality work in design, writing, coding, and more.

This chapter will help you start your freelance journey using AI — with real platforms, tools, and strategies.

1. Why Freelancing with AI is a Smart Move

Problem Faced by Students	AI-Enabled Solution
No professional portfolio	Use Canva or Notion AI to build one fast
Lack of experience	Let AI improve output and speed up delivery
Can't find clients	Use Fiverr/Upwork with AI-enhanced proposals
Don't know what to offer	AI suggests trending services (e.g., logos, blogs, resumes)

2. Top Platforms to Start Freelancing

Fiverr – Sell Any AI-Powered Skill

* Offer services like resume writing (Rezi), AI-generated art (DALL·E), or summaries (ChatGPT)
* Create gig titles and descriptions with Copy.ai or ChatGPT

2. Upwork – Long-Term Freelance Projects

* Apply to tech projects using a strong proposal
* Use AI to draft cover letters, proposals, and even solutions

3. Freelancer.com / PeoplePerHour

* Smaller, quicker projects ideal for students
* AI helps complete basic tasks faster (design, research, scripting)

3. Best AI Tools to Boost Freelance Work

Service / Niche	AI Tools to Use
Logo or Brand Design	Canva AI, Looka, Adobe Firefly
Article Writing	Jasper.ai, Copy.ai, ChatGPT
Coding Projects	GitHub Copilot, Replit AI
Video Editing	Pictory, RunwayML, Pika Labs
Data Entry/Analysis	ChatGPT + Excel + AI spreadsheet tools

🎓 Real Student Use Cases

* An AI/ML student used **Jasper** to write blogs and earned ₹20,000/month on Fiverr
* An ECE student built **mini websites using Replit AI** and got repeat clients from Upwork
* A mechanical student offered **3D modeling using AI tools** for prototypes and designs

📌 Case Study: From College to Client

Name: Rakesh (CSE, 4th Year)
Skills: Web development + AI tools
Platform Used: Fiverr + GitHub Copilot + ChatGPT

Outcome:

- Built over 30 websites with AI-assisted tools
- Generated monthly income of ₹40,000+ and used the earnings to fund personal projects

🖼 Screenshot / Visualization Ideas

- ✓ Fiverr gig made using AI-generated banner
- ✓ ChatGPT writing proposal for a freelancing job
- ✓ Jasper dashboard with published content samples

🔮 Future Outlook: Freelancing x AI

Trend	What's Coming
AI-Powered Freelance Portals	Smart platforms match students to best-fit clients
AI Skill Certifications	Verified AI proficiency badges to improve credibility
Micro-Freelancing	Delivering mini-tasks in under 1 hour with AI
AI Collectives	Student teams powered by AI tools for joint freelance projects

🧠 Reflect & Research Exercises

1. **Sign up on Fiverr or Upwork** and create your first AI gig
2. **Use ChatGPT or Copy.ai** to write a 3-line bio + 1 project description
3. **Find 3 trending freelance services** that can be delivered using AI
4. **Interview a freelancer** and ask how AI is changing their work speed or quality

🎓 Why This Chapter Matters for B.Tech Students

Freelancing with AI is more than income — it's experience, visibility, and a smart career step.

* Build your portfolio while earning
* Learn by doing real projects
* Turn your AI skills into assets

💰 Use your laptop not just to learn — but to earn.

Chapter 33: Monetizing AI Knowledge: YouTube, eBooks & Online Courses

Introduction

As the world becomes more AI-driven, students and professionals can transform their AI knowledge into income streams. This chapter explores how to leverage platforms like YouTube, Amazon Kindle, and course platforms like Udemy, Skillshare, and Teachable to monetize what you know about AI.

Real-Time Examples of AI Tools

Platform	Purpose	AI Tool to Assist
YouTube	Video content creation	Pictory, Descript, Synthesia, ChatGPT for scripting
eBooks	Writing and publishing	ChatGPT, Grammarly, Canva, Reedsy
Online Courses	Course creation and marketing	Notion, ChatGPT, Canva, Tella, Teachable, Loom

How to Monetize AI Knowledge – Step-by-Step

➢ Start a YouTube Channel

Niche: Focus on "AI for Students" or "AI Tools Tutorials"
Content Ideas:

- ✓ "Top 5 AI Tools for Students in 2025"
- ✓ "How to Automate Assignments using ChatGPT"

Use AI Tools:

- ✓ ChatGPT for scriptwriting
- ✓ Pictory or Descript to convert text to video Canva or Thumbnail.AI for engaging thumbnails

Monetization:

- ✓ Google AdSense (after 1,000 subs and 4,000 hours watch time) Affiliate marketing using AI tool links
- ✓ Sponsored content

Topic Examples:

AI Tools Workflow:

- ✓ ChatGPT for drafting Grammarly for grammar check
- ✓ Canva or Reedsy for design and formatting

Publishing:

- Amazon Kindle Direct Publishing (KDP) Gumroad or Payhip for direct selling

Promotion:

- Instagram Reels LinkedIn posts
- Telegram channels or YouTube mentions
-

➢ **Launch an Online Course Course Topics:**

"AI Tools for College Productivity"

"Build AI Projects Using No-Code Tools"

Structure:

- Use Notion to plan lessons
- Use Loom or OBS to record lectures
- Use Tella or Canva for slides

Platforms:

- Udemy, Skillshare (ready traffic)
- Teachable, Thinkific (self-brand)

Monetization:

Passive income per sale

Bundle with eBooks or community access

📌 Case Study: A B.Tech Student Monetizing AI

Name: Mehul, Final Year ECE Student

Action: Started a YouTube channel on AI tool tutorials.

Used ChatGPT to write scripts and Pictory to generate videos. Cross-promoted his eBook "AI for College Projects" on his channel.

Result:

* 15,000 YouTube subscribers in 6 months
* ₹20,000/month from affiliate links and eBook sales Launched his first Skillshare course on "AI for Engineers"

🖼 Visual/Infographic Suggestions

- A funnel diagram: Knowledge → Content → Monetization
- Timeline graphic: April → YouTube → June → eBook → August → Course
- A comparison chart: YouTube vs eBook vs Online Course monetization models

🔮 Future Outlook

The creator economy is shifting towards knowledge monetization. In 2025 and beyond, students with even basic AI skills can turn into edupreneurs. Tools like Sora (AI video generation) will further simplify content creation, making it even easier to earn by teaching AI.

🧠 Exercises & Research Prompts

- Create a 3-video content plan for a YouTube channel on AI tools. Outline your first AI-based eBook (title, chapters, target readers).
- Choose a topic and create a course syllabus using Notion or Google Docs.
- Research 2 creators who make money teaching AI and analyze their model.

- Draft your affiliate links page for AI tools you use (use Gumroad or Carrd).

🎯 why this chapter for B.Tech Students

Build passive income while still studying

Stand out in placements by demonstrating personal branding
Learn entrepreneurial, marketing, and communication skills
Practical application of your AI learning into real-world value

---

Part 7: Learning by Doing

Encourage hands-on exploration and continuous self-learning

Chapter 34: How to Build Your First AI App

From Idea to Innovation — Create Your First AI App Step-by-Step

Introduction

Learning AI is one thing, but building something real with it is what truly unlocks its power. This chapter is your **hands-on guide** to build your very first AI-powered app — even with basic coding knowledge. Whether it's a chatbot, image classifier, or simple voice assistant, this is your launchpad into AI development.

1. What You'll Need (Tools Checklist)

Requirement	Suggested Tools
Programming	Python (or JavaScript for web-based apps)
Code Editor	VS Code, Replit, or Google Colab
AI Libraries	OpenAI API, Hugging Face, TensorFlow, scikit-learn
Interface (UI)	Streamlit, Flask, Gradio
Hosting (optional)	GitHub Pages, Heroku, Render

2. Choosing an AI App Idea (Simple Yet Useful)

Beginner-Friendly App Ideas:

- ✓ AI **Chatbot** using OpenAI (e.g., a study help bot)
- ✓ AI **Image Classifier** (e.g., detect fruits, electronics, or traffic signs)

- ✓ AI **Resume Evaluator** (input resume PDF → get suggestions)
- ✓ AI **Quiz Generator** from textbook PDFs
- ✓ AI **Voice Assistant** using Speech Recognition + OpenAI

3. Step-by-Step: Build an AI Chatbot App

Let's build:"**StudyBuddy" – an AI-powered study helper chatbot**

- ➢ **Install Requirements:**

```bash
pip install openai streamlit
```

- ➢ **Create Your App File:** `studybuddy.py`

```python
import openai
import streamlit as st

openai.api_key = 'YOUR-API-KEY'

st.title("📚 StudyBuddy - Ask Anything")
user_input = st.text_input("Ask your question:")

if user_input:
response = openai.ChatCompletion.create( model="gpt-3.5-turbo",
messages=[{"role": "user", "content": user_input}]
```

)
st.write("Response:",response["choices"][0]["message"]["content"])

➢ **Run the App:**

```bash
streamlit run studybuddy.py
```

➢ **What It Does:**

* Accepts student's questions
* Returns helpful answers using ChatGPT
* Simple, interactive web interface

4. Bonus: Add Features

Feature	How to Add
Save chat history	Use `st.session_state` in Streamlit
Voice Input	Use `SpeechRecognition` Python library
File Upload	Let users upload syllabus PDF and use OCR to parse content
Dark Mode	Customize with Streamlit themes

Reflect & Experiment

* Modify the app to become a **Subject-specific Tutor Bot**
* Add MCQ quiz generation
* Train your own custom model for a specific task (like medical Q\&A)

Screenshot Ideas

* Streamlit app running locally
* Code snippet in VS Code
* User asking questions and getting responses

🔮 Future Possibilities

Direction	Example Outcome
Add NLP Understanding	Use LangChain or RAG for document-based Q&A
Make it Multilingual	Add translation layer for regional language support
Deploy on Web	Use Heroku or Render to share the app online
Turn into a Startup	Offer study-assistance service for exam prep companies

🧠 Exercises

1. Build your own version of StudyBuddy using any interface (Flask, Gradio, etc.)
2. Use Hugging Face to build a small image classifier app
3. Record a screen demo of your app and share on GitHub or LinkedIn
4. Ask ChatGPT: "How can I improve this AI chatbot for students?"

🎓 Why This Chapter Matters for B.Tech Students

You move from consumer to **creator**. This is where your AI journey becomes practical.

* You learn API calls, interfaces, and user experience
* You gain confidence by showing real work
* This is portfolio gold — your app speaks louder than your resume

🚀 Start simple. Learn fast. Build smart.

Chapter 35: Top 10 Mini Projects with AI — Challenge Yourself to Create More

Learn by Building — Real AI Projects for Practice & Portfolio

Introduction

Mini projects are like the gym for your AI skills — small, intense, and results-driven. They help you explore real-world applications of AI, improve your problem-solving abilities, and build an impressive portfolio.

In this chapter, we present **10 mini projects** that any B.Tech student (with basic programming knowledge) can build using AI tools and APIs.

➢ Top 10 AI Mini Project Ideas

1.AI-Powered MCQ Generator

- ✓ Input: PDF textbook or notes
- ✓ Output: Multiple-choice questions
- ✓ Tools: Python, OCR (Tesseract), OpenAI API

2. AI Resume Reviewer

- ✓ Upload a resume and get improvement suggestions
- ✓ Tools: Streamlit, ChatGPT API, PDF Reader

3. Smart Image Classifier

- ✓ Classify dog breeds, fruits, electronics, etc.
- ✓ Tools: TensorFlow/Keras + Python GUI (Tkinter or Streamlit)

4. AI Exam Timer + Focus App

- ✓ Detects if the user is distracted during online study
- ✓ Tools: OpenCV, face detection, Python

5. Sentiment Analyzer for YouTube Comments

- ✓ Input: URL of video
- ✓ Output: Sentiment breakdown (positive/neutral/negative)
- ✓ Tools: Python, YouTube API, TextBlob or Hugging Face

6. Voice-Based Assistant

- ✓ Takes voice input, returns AI-powered answers
- ✓ Tools: SpeechRecognition, OpenAI, Pyttsx3

7. AI Code Reviewer

- ✓ Upload Python code, get suggestions and comments
- ✓ Tools: ChatGPT API + CodeMirror interface

8. Instagram Caption Generator

- ✓ Suggest captions based on uploaded image
- ✓ Tools: DALL·E, CLIP + GPT (vision-text pipeline)

9. Career Recommendation Bot

- ✓ Ask questions and get career options based on interests
- ✓ Tools: Streamlit + OpenAI

10. Mini Chatbot with Memory

- ✓ Simple chatbot that remembers user context during a session
- ✓ Tools: LangChain + OpenAI + Streamlit

Project Tips

1. Start with 1 feature. Expand as you learn.
2. Focus on user interface (UI) — even simple apps feel premium with good UX.
3. Share your projects on GitHub, LinkedIn, or personal websites.
4. Reuse templates like Streamlit or Flask to speed up development.

🖼 Screenshot / Visualization Ideas

* Dashboards, code UI, or feature output screenshots
* Flowcharts or data pipelines for each project
*

🧠 Exercises

1. Pick 2 projects and make a plan (tools, features, goal)
2. Build one project this weekend and present it in class or online
3. Join GitHub, upload your project, and write a good README
4. Ask ChatGPT to test your project and suggest improvements

🎓 Why This Chapter Matters for B.Tech Students

Mini projects are proof that you can apply your AI knowledge.

* Recruiters want to see initiative
* Projects = hands-on skills
* They make you stand out in placements, hackathons, and interviews

🛠 These 10 projects are just the beginning. Your portfolio is your playground.

Chapter 36: How to Use APIs of OpenAI, Google Cloud, Hugging Face

Power Up Your Projects — Connecting to the World's Best AI Models with APIs

Introduction

AI APIs give you **access to powerful models** without needing to train them yourself. Whether it's generating text with OpenAI, translating languages with Google Cloud, or analyzing sentiment using Hugging Face, APIs make AI accessible to every B.Tech student.

In this chapter, you'll learn:

- ❖ What an API is
- ❖ How to get API keys
- ❖ How to use APIs from OpenAI, Google Cloud, and Hugging Face in simple projects

1. What is an API?

API = Application Programming Interface

It's a bridge that allows one software to talk to another. Think of it like ordering food from a restaurant:

- ✓ You (app) place the order (API call)
- ✓ The kitchen (AI model) prepares it
- ✓ You receive the dish (response)

Why Use APIs in AI?

* No need for high-end computing or training
* Use powerful models instantly
* Save time and effort

2. Getting API Keys (Step-by-Step)

- **OpenAI API Key**
  1. Visit:https://platform.openai.com/
  2. Create an account → Click on 'API Keys'
  3. Copy your secret key (keep it private!)

- **Google Cloud API Key**
  1. Visit:https://console.cloud.google.com/
  2. Create a new project → Enable desired API (like Translate API)
  3. Go to Credentials → Generate API Key

- **Hugging Face Token**
  1. Visit: https://huggingface.co/
  2. Create an account → Go to Settings → Access Tokens
  3. Generate a 'Read' token for free access to public models

3. Example: Using OpenAI API in Python

```python
import openai

openai.api_key = 'your_api_key_here'

response = openai.ChatCompletion.create( model="gpt-3.5-turbo",
messages=[{"role": "user", "content": "Explain AI in simple terms"}]
)
print(response["choices"][0]["message"]["content"])
```

Output:

A clear AI explanation in seconds!

4. Using Google Cloud Translate API

```python
from google.cloud import translate_v2 as translate client =
translate.Client()

result = client.translate('Hello World',
target_language='te') print(result['translatedText'])
```

Output: “హలో వరe5C, ” (in Telugu)

5. Using Hugging Face Transformers (Sentiment Analysis)

```python
from transformers import pipeline

classifier = pipeline('sentiment-analysis') result =
classifier("AI is amazing!") print(result)
```

Output: \[{'label': 'POSITIVE', 'score': 0.999...}]

Project Ideas Using APIs

API Used	Project Idea
OpenAI	AI Q&A chatbot for B.Tech subjects
Google Cloud	Language translator for campus projects
Hugging Face	Sentiment analysis for app reviews

📷 Screenshot / Visual Ideas

* API dashboard showing usage
* Code + Output of API in a notebook
* Hugging Face model explorer

🧠 Exercises

1. Sign up for all three platforms and generate API keys
2. Build a basic chatbot using OpenAI API
3. Use Google Translate API to localize your app into two languages
4. Run a Hugging Face model for sentiment, summarization, or translation

🎓 Why This Chapter Matters for B.Tech Students

API integration is a **must-have tech skill**. It connects your project to the global AI ecosystem.

* You don't need to build everything from scratch
* Saves time, adds power, increases value

🔌 With APIs, you don't just learn AI — you deploy it.

Chapter 37: Building a Portfolio Using AI Tools — Stand Out with Smart Work

From Learner to Leader — Use AI to Create a Stunning Tech Portfolio

Introduction

A strong portfolio showcases your skills better than a resume ever could. It reflects your projects, personality, and growth. With AI tools, building an attractive, impactful portfolio has never been easier — even if you aren't a design expert or web developer.

This chapter will guide you step-by-step on how to create a **portfolio that speaks volumes**, using AI to design, write, and present your best work.

1. What to Include in a Tech Portfolio

Section	What to Add
About Me	Short intro + your passion for AI/tech
Projects	Title, description, tools used, screenshots, GitHub links
Skills & Tools	List of AI tools, libraries, platforms you've used
Certifications	Free AI course certificates (Coursera, Google, etc.)
Blogs/Videos	YouTube tutorials or LinkedIn blogs on AI topics
Contact Links	Email, LinkedIn, GitHub, etc.

2. AI Tools to Build a Portfolio

Tool	Use Case
Notion	Build a portfolio site with templates
Carrd / Webflow	No-code site builders for sleek designs
Canva AI	Design logos, project thumbnails, banners
ChatGPT	Write "About Me," project descriptions, summaries
GitHub Copilot	Help with README.md files or documentation

3. Steps to Create Your Portfolio Website

Step 1: Plan Content

* List 4–5 of your best projects
* Gather screenshots, GitHub links, descriptions

Step 2: Choose a Platform

* Use **Notion** or **Carrd** for quick setup
* Use **GitHub Pages** if comfortable with HTML/Markdown

Step 3: Use ChatGPT to Write

* Prompt: "Write a project summary for an AI quiz generator built in Python."*
* Use the response in your portfolio page

Step 4: Add Visuals

* Design a banner in Canva AI: *"Create a tech-themed portfolio header for a student"* Step 5: Publish & Share
* Share the link in resumes, job applications, LinkedIn

Extra Sections to Impress

Add-On Section	Why It Matters
Testimonials	Classmates or mentors vouch for your work
Project Demos (GIFs)	Visual walkthroughs stand out more than screenshots
Research/Whitepapers	Highlight academic credibility
Hackathon Achievements	Shows you solve real-world problems

Reflect & Improve

- Ask ChatGPT to review your portfolio like a recruiter
- Run Grammarly on all your text content for polish
- Use Replit or Streamlit to embed working projects in real-time

Screenshot / Visualization Ideas

* Portfolio homepage sample
* Project tile layout
* Before/after using Canva AI for visuals

Exercises

1. Draft your portfolio homepage content using ChatGPT
2. Create a free website using Notion or GitHub Pages
3. Add 3 projects with description + screenshot
4. Ask 2 classmates to review and give feedback

🎓 Why This Chapter Matters for B.Tech Students

Your portfolio is **proof of work**. It speaks when you aren't in the room.

* Projects prove your skills
* AI tools make it professional and presentable
* Every recruiter, mentor, or investor looks for a link — give them a reason to click

🌐 Build it once, keep updating, and let your portfolio win opportunities for you.

Chapter 38: Competitions & Hackathons — How to Win with AI

AI + Innovation = Victory — Succeed in Hackathons and Challenges

Introduction

Hackathons and AI competitions are **launchpads for innovation**. They push your limits, grow your network, and boost your resume. Whether online or on campus, AI-powered ideas are now winning most hackathons.

This chapter shows how to:

- Find the best hackathons
- Use AI tools to solve real-world problems
- Prepare, present, and win as a team or solo participant

1. Where to Find AI Competitions

Platform	Description
Devpost.com	Global hackathons (college-friendly)
Kaggle.com	Data science + AI competitions
Hackerearth.com	Coding + innovation challenges
Smart India Hackathon	National-level student innovation platform
College/Techfest Events	On-campus hackathons (check CSE/ECE clubs)

2. How to Use AI in a Hackathon Project

Use Case	AI Tool / Library Example
Summarizing problems	ChatGPT, Gemini
Predictive modeling	scikit-learn, TensorFlow
Sentiment analysis	Hugging Face transformers
Image detection	OpenCV, YOLO, MediaPipe
Data visualization	Tableau AI, PowerBI, Python (matplotlib)

3. Idea Blueprint for Hackathon Teams

Project: AI Safety Monitor for College Labs

- ✓ Sensors + Camera detect unsafe behavior
- ✓ AI model raises real-time alerts
- ✓ Dashboard logs incidents for safety auditing

Tools: OpenCV + Python + Streamlit + ChatGPT (for idea refinement)

4. AI Tools to Speed Up Your Project

Task	AI Tool Suggestion
Idea generation	ChatGPT, FutureTools.io
Writing documentation	Notion AI, Grammarly
Code suggestions	GitHub Copilot, Tabnine
Pitch deck design	Tome AI, Canva AI
Presentation rehearsals	Yoodli AI, Presentations.ai

5. Tips to Win

- ✓ **Problem First:** Don't chase fancy AI — solve a real pain point.
- ✓ **Keep it Simple:** Judges prefer usable over complex.
- ✓ **Show a Demo:** Even a basic prototype is powerful.

✓ **Tell a Story:** Use AI-generated visuals to craft your pitch.
✓ **Team Matters:** Combine coders, designers, presenters.

📷 Screenshot / Visualization Ideas

* Hackathon dashboard
* Demo app screenshot
* AI-generated pitch deck slide sample

🧠 Exercises

1. Register for a hackathon in the next 30 days
2. Use ChatGPT to brainstorm 3 AI-based ideas
3. Build a 3-slide pitch using Tome AI or Canva
4. Collaborate with 2 peers to form a mini hackathon team

🎓 Why This Chapter Matters for B.Tech Students

Hackathons help you:

* Apply classroom knowledge to real problems
* Work in teams (essential for jobs/startups)
* Build fast under pressure
* Network with recruiters, mentors, innovators

🏆 Winning is great, but **participation alone sets you apart**
Use AI to build smarter, faster, better.

Chapter 39: Final Summary — Becoming a Smart AI Student

From Learner to Leader — Your AI Journey Starts Now

Introduction

You've reached the final chapter of your AI journey through this eBook. From understanding what AI is to building your own apps, using tools in academics, innovation, health, and careers — you've gained not just knowledge but also practical power. Now it's time to summarize, reflect, and prepare to act.

What You've Learned in This Book

Part	Focus Area	Key Takeaways
1	AI Basics	History, types, and future of AI
2	AI in Academics	AI tools for study, coding, presentations
3	AI for Projects	Innovation tools, no-code apps, real-world examples
4	AI for Personal Growth	Tools for mental health, fitness, productivity
5	AI in Creativity & Careers	Resume writing, freelancing, monetizing skills
6	Learning by Doing	Mini-projects, APIs, portfolio building, hackathons
7	B.Tech AI Subject Essentials	Syllabus, labs, viva, and learning paths

How to Think Like a Smart AI Student

Be Curious – Always ask how AI can solve everyday problems.
Be Practical – Learn by doing, not just reading.
Be Ethical – Use AI responsibly and fairly.
Be Collaborative – AI is a team sport — build with others.
Be Future-Ready – New tools come fast — stay updated.

📅 30-Day Smart AI Student Action Plan

Week Action Step

- ❖ Set up Notion + build a study planner using AI tools
- ❖ Start 1 mini-project (choose from this book)
- ❖ Build your AI portfolio website + share on LinkedIn
- ❖ Register for 1 AI hackathon or competition

🔮 Your AI Future

Build your LinkedIn + GitHub presence.

Write blogs on Medium or Hashnode using AI. Create YouTube tutorials using Tome AI + Canva.

Apply for internships in AI or data roles.

💬 "Don't just be a user of AI — become a creator."

Final Reflection Exercise

- What was your favorite tool or idea from the book?
- Which 3 projects will you complete in the next 2 months?
- Write your AI mission statement: **"I will use AI to…"**

🎓 Why This Chapter Matters for B.Tech Students

This chapter helps you consolidate all your learning and take the next step. Whether it's preparing for placements, launching a startup, or pursuing higher studies, AI gives you the edge.

From theory to practical, from student to innovator — you are now a Smart AI Student.

Thank you for reading!

Go build something amazing with AI. Your journey doesn't end here — it begins here.